DELUDED BY DAW

Deluded
by
Dawkins?

A Christian Response to
The God Delusion

ANDREW J. WILSON

KINGSWAY PUBLICATIONS
EASTBOURNE

Quotations from the Bible are from
the English Standard Version (ESV)
© 2001 by Crossway Bibles,
a division of Good News Publishers.

ISBN 978–1–84291–355–0

Cover design by Pinnacle Creative
Typeset by Alliance Interactive Technology

4 5 6 7 Printing/Year 10 09 08 07

Published by
KINGSWAY COMMUNICATIONS LTD
Lottbridge Drove, Eastbourne BN23 6NT, England.
books@kingsway.co.uk
Printed in Great Britain

Contents

Preface and Acknowledgements

Christianity has always faced opposition and ridicule. From AD 30 onwards, the sect of people who proclaimed the resurrection of Jesus were accused of being dangerous, delirious, delinquent and deluded. They were often hounded, persecuted and even killed for their beliefs. Yet rather than hide away in Christian ghettos, the early church made a habit of going straight into the lion's den – the Jerusalem Temple, the Ephesian debate hall, the Athenian marketplace, the Roman Colosseum – and picking fights. They did this because of a conviction that what they were preaching and living was *true*, and that they therefore had nothing to fear from debating it publicly. And so the world changed.

It is with that in mind that I have written this book as a specific response to Richard Dawkins' latest bestseller, *The God Delusion*. My intention is not to stop books like *The God Delusion* from being written, nor to pour scorn on those who read them. My aim, rather, is to highlight the dangers of reading them uncritically. In a world where mockery and argument can often get confused, it is important to sift what we read, whether we are Christians or not: to find out what is true, respond appropriately, and reject what is false. Watching an intelligent and articulate man marshal every argument he and his army of colleagues can find, from a lifetime debating these issues, can be very challenging. But fight is better than flight (or, even worse, fright). So *Deluded by Dawkins?* meets Richard Dawkins head-on, for better or worse, and subjects his book to some serious scrutiny.

The material in this book was entirely shaped and written while working at Kings Church in Eastbourne, and was originally intended to be posted as an article on the church website (www.kingschurch.eu). As a book it will no doubt have its flaws, but hopefully unreality, in the sense of being divorced from the questions real people ask, will not be one of them. I am deeply grateful, once again, for the privilege of being and working in a church where time is set aside for me to write, with the aim of equipping Christians to preach the gospel. I was unwittingly prompted to write this book by Alison Gamester, and was encouraged to develop it by the elders at Kings: Graham Marsh and Dave Dean. Sam Arnold and my whole Life Group have prayed for me through the process. I have also received encouragement, feedback and improvements from Julian Adams, Phil Moore, Nick Chatrath, Phil James, John Groves, Joel Virgo, Guy Miller and particularly Liam Thatcher, along with many of my Impact students. Finally, the preparation of the book for publication – and indeed the idea of publishing it at all – is entirely the work of my editor Richard Herkes who, with Sue Price and Dave Roberts, has conjured this book out of thin air in a very short space of time. I would like to thank all of them for their enthusiasm, interest and support.

However, it is Rachel, my wife, who should get the most credit (if that is what it is!) for what follows. When lost in the detail of the arguments, and frustrated with myself for not being able to grapple with all of them, she has continually encouraged me and prayed for me and laughed at me. Again and again, she has reminded me that a book like this has the potential to help people: puzzled agnostics, preoccupied students, Alpha Course hosts, youth workers, and even card-carrying atheists.

So I hope it will!

Andrew Wilson

Introduction

A Case of Overconfidence?

When George Bush was running for president, he was interviewed by Andy Hiller in New Hampshire. The political reporter asked him if he could name the leaders of four hotspots around the world: Taiwan, Chechnya, India and Pakistan. Bush got Taiwan right, made no attempt at Chechnya or India, and his response to Pakistan brought about the widely-quoted response, 'General. I can name the general, General.' Irritated at being tested like a schoolboy, Bush then asked Hiller if he could name the Mexican foreign minister. 'No sir,' Hiller replied, 'but I would say to that, I'm not running for president.'

Richard Dawkins has spent much of his career attacking belief in God, particularly the Christian God. He has written books about it, made television shows about it, and travelled the world debating it, and even before the publication of *The God Delusion*, was probably the world's most high-profile atheist. Yet when described by his fellow Oxford professor Alister McGrath as largely ignorant of Christian theology, Dawkins responded:

'I imagine that McGrath would join me in expressing disbelief in fairies, astrology and Thor's hammer. How would he respond if a fairyologist, astrologer or Viking accused him of ignorance of their respective subjects?'[1]

Were Andy Hiller the interviewer, he might well have responded as he did to George Bush: McGrath was not trying to prove these entities did not exist! It is no good attempting to overturn belief in God while at the same time openly confessing massive ignorance of such belief. No debate as important as the existence of God will ever be settled by people who show such disdain for the opposition, particularly when it means they have such limited knowledge of their subject matter that they litter their works with errors (as Dawkins would no doubt say of many creationists).[2] As an atheist, he may well consider ignorance – of Christian origins, the Bible, the evidence for the resurrection and so on – to be bliss. But he should not expect the rest of us to take him seriously if he does.

---

[1] *Science and Theology News*, 25th April 2005. Dawkins, like everyone, hates being misquoted, so it should be said that the above quotation was preceded by the words, 'I have, of course, met this point before. It sounds superficially fair. But it presupposes that that there is something in Christian theology to be ignorant about. The entire thrust of my position is that Christian theology is a non-subject. It is empty. Vacuous. Devoid of coherence or content.' This may explain his otherwise curious ignorance on a number of key historical facts that are relevant to the thesis of *The God Delusion*.

[2] On errors in *The God Delusion*, see following chapters, especially the section on Scripture.

The one who states his case first seems right, until the other comes and examines him.

Proverbs 18:17

1

Throwing Down the Gauntlet

Many believers are grateful to Richard Dawkins, but for the wrong reasons. Some have rejoiced that the belligerence of his case will make many agnostics recoil in distaste, making theism more potentially attractive. Others have celebrated his forays into areas of which he appears largely ignorant, because it means he has overreached himself, in the manner of a 1960s radical feminist or a 1980s militant environmentalist, and has thereby tarnished or even undermined many of the undoubtedly good points he makes. Both reactions, however, miss the point. Belligerence and overreach may have unfortunate side-effects, but the book remains a clear, provocative and witty plague on all our houses, and it is no more aggressive or overconfident than a number of theistic equivalents. The chief reason Christians should be grateful to Dawkins is this: he has gathered together all of the best arguments against God's existence into one place, with the intention of debating them publicly.

To do so has taken courage. Although he may protest too much on behalf of the poor oppressed atheistic minority who have been wickedly excluded from political clout by being too educated to agree with each other,[1] he has frequently been bold enough to articulate what nobody else would, in America as elsewhere, and I would not wish his hate mail on anybody.[2] More importantly, however, it has taken a vital realisation, which Dawkins, like the apostle Paul, has experienced, but which many others (both atheists and theists) have not: that like all other worldviews, religious ones deserve to be discussed, debated and decided publicly. I cannot imagine anyone finishing *The God Delusion* and regarding their faith as a private matter which cannot influence or be influenced by the outside world, any more than I can imagine anyone leaving Paul's debates in the lecture hall of Tyrannus with the same misconception.[3] Beliefs, any beliefs, should be debated in the open.

That is the central challenge of *The God Delusion*, and it

---

[1] Dawkins, *The God Delusion* (London: Bantam Press 2006), pp. 4–5. Cf. too pp. 43–45, where he asks, 'What might American atheists achieve if they organized themselves properly?' Without in any way endorsing the shocking abuses he seeks to address in these pages, one wonders whether the desire for atheists to have greater political welly has skewed his presentation (it is otherwise hard to see how this particular excursus contributes to his argument about the non-existence of God).

[2] As listed in Dawkins, pp. 211–214.

[3] Acts 19:8–10; cf. also 6:9–10; 9:22, 29; 17:2–3, 17–32; 18:4; 26:24–29.

should be celebrated by Christians. The internal bubble of private piety, which owes something to the Reformation, something to the Enlightenment, something to the Victorian period, and nothing at all to the Bible, is as resoundingly burst by the book of Acts as by Dawkins. And if the reviews are right, and the world's leading atheist has actually published the definitive statement of the world's best atheistic arguments, then the modern believer can be reasonably confident that, having struggled with Dawkins and overcome, they are unlikely to find their faith overturned by anything else, even if they get their hip put out of joint in the process.[4] As Elijah demonstrated, it is easier to confute sceptics if you have all your targets in one place.[5]

This is not to say that, as a statement of the arguments for atheism, the book is without flaws. Some may laud Dawkins' familiarly arrogant style as fresh, and it certainly makes the book more saleable, but there is nothing clever about implying from the outset that those who disagree with you are 'dyed-in-the-wool faith-heads',

---

[4] Genesis 32:24–28. As I shall argue, there are a number of components of Dawkins' argument that should be taken seriously by the church as a whole.

[5] 1 Kings 18:19 and following. This story is one of countless biblical examples of belief in God being based on empirical evidence, not on the sort of philosophical game-playing that Dawkins rightly snorts at in Chapter 3: 'the God who answers by fire, he is God' (1 Kings 18:24). Old Testament Jews and New Testament Christians seem, in this respect, to have been rather more hard-headed than many of their medieval or modern counterparts.

'immune to argument' as a result of 'childhood indoctrination',[6] especially since several of the last half-century's most influential Christian debaters have been converted atheists and sceptics.[7] His irreverence, though unsurprising given his beliefs, is also quite trying (and tiring) in places, and seems to be intended to make unbelievers laugh and believers wince; in the latter he has succeeded, although perhaps not in the sense he intended.[8] Neither of these things undermines his case with those who already agree with him, of course, but that is no reason to write them.

---

[6] Dawkins, p. 5.

[7] So, famously, C. S. Lewis, who deserves better than to be summarily dismissed in less than a paragraph (Dawkins, p. 92), on which see below; Dawkins' Oxford contemporary Alister McGrath, also all-but-ignored by Dawkins, despite the huge relevance and impressive scholarship of his recent book *The Twilight of Atheism* (London: Random House 2004), which Dawkins never mentions; Ravi Zacharias, whose arguments in books like *Can Man Live Without God?* (Dallas: Word 2004) are, again, ignored; Lee Strobel, whose *The Case for a Creator* (Grand Rapids: Zondervan 2004) and *The Case for Christ* (Grand Rapids: Zondervan 1998) are bestsellers of Christian apologetics at a popular level; and so on.

[8] E.g. Dawkins, p. 31; open debate is one thing, but aiming to offend is another. In years of reading Christian books, I have never read an attack on any belief system that even approaches this page in terms of vitriol, and therefore his use of the word 'insouciant' to describe the Catholic Encyclopedia on the following page was, I hope, ironic. My wince of response was thus not one of doubt, but of compassion and concern – a combination of Luke 23:34 and 23:40, if you will.

Rather more problematic than stylistic quibbles are issues at the argumentative level. These include his lack of even-handedness (for example, stating that when theists of previous centuries did good things, theism cannot be credited because everyone believed in God, but when they did bad things, theism gets all the blame);[9] his very limited understanding of New Testament studies, which although understandable, does somewhat cloud his attempt to explain Christian origins;[10] and his inaccuracies (of which the most amusing example is his assertion that Thomas Jefferson, who died in 1826, was telling his nephew to read the

---

[9] Compare, for instance, Dawkins, p. 86 ('it was pretty much the only option in their time') and p. 98 ('Newton did indeed claim to be religious. So did almost everybody') with the blaming of religion for witch-hunts, Crusades, the Gunpowder Plot, the Inquisition, and so on. Whether any of the latter, of for that matter the former, were disciples in the sense Jesus or the apostles would have understood it is not considered. It is perhaps not impertinent to suggest that killing people in the name of God back then (and in many places to this day) was akin to killing people in the name of empire in the nineteenth century, or democracy in the twenty-first. The means do not always vitiate the end.

[10] The only two New Testament scholars Dawkins quotes or refers to are Geza Vermes and Bart Ehrman, who interestingly happen to be two of only three New Testament scholars I can find in my local Waterstone's bookshop. The third is ironically N. T. Wright, whose work, had Dawkins engaged with it (read it?), would have helped him significantly on the question of Christian origins.

'Gospels' of Thomas, Philip, and Mary Magdalen,
which all readers of *The Da Vinci Code* know were not
discovered until 1945. If Dawkins is right, then Jefferson had a prophetic gift which would presumably
undermine his central hypothesis anyway.) More substantial errors, and simplifications so dramatic that they
significantly mislead, will be addressed in more detail
as we continue.

Most seriously, Dawkins spends the best part of the
book either making points that are not directly relevant
to the question of whether or not there is a god (see next
section), or attacking bad reasons to believe that there is,
while the most definitive argument that Christians have
used since AD 30, the resurrection of Jesus, is not even
discussed.[11] From the point of view of Christian preaching, both in the Bible and throughout church history, the
resurrection is the elephant in the room, the one giant
that has to be felled if Christianity is to be buried.[12]
Despite seventeen centuries of sceptics from Celsus to
Crossan, no plausible alternative explanation has ever
been articulated, as we shall see, and it is damaging to

---

[11] Mysteriously, this is often true of atheist writers; see also
Daniel Dennett, *Breaking the Spell:* Religion as a Natural Phenomenon (London: Penguin, 2006), pp. 240–249. Dennett is a
remarkable philosopher, but rivals Dawkins in his misunder-
standing of the basis for Christian theism, and his bravado in dismissing the existence of God in the space of nine (somewhat
inadequate) pages.

[12] 1 Corinthians 15:14.

Dawkins' argument, perhaps fatally so, that he never examines it.

There are some reasons for this, no doubt. Perhaps he believes that his anti-supernaturalist argument is strong enough to settle the issue without looking at the evidence. Perhaps he assumes that his largely sceptical readership will not notice, which may well be true. Perhaps he is aware that a historical minefield awaits those who try to explain the resurrection in rationalist terms – the resurrection is to materialists what satellite photos are to the Flat Earth Society. Or perhaps, to put it no stronger, he is not really prepared to engage with the worldview-challenging events of Easter, save to say that they cannot have happened because dead people don't rise. If so, his position is just as unquestioning, just as fundamentalist, as that of many of the individuals he has written his book to refute.

That said, *The God Delusion* is a stimulating book, and one that has deservedly received attention. Standing on the shoulders of Dawkins' previous works, it makes as convincing a case as can be made for atheism, integrating biblical, historical, moral, sociological and scientific arguments in a sustained polemic against belief in any god, particularly the Christian God. It also combines unusually wide-ranging content with an elegant and amusing style, which makes the writing compelling entertainment, whatever one thinks of the argument. If any book were able to shake the faithful and rally the faithless, it would be this one. Happily, whether or not it

does the latter, it looks unlikely to achieve the former.[13]
In the rest of this book, we shall see why.

---

[13] That the book looks certain to face some resounding
raspberries from the evangelical world (and not just the ignorant
fundamentalists Dawkins hates so much) is implied by the 14,000
hits I got on Google for "The Dawkins Delusion", and also by the
fact that some scientific and theological heavyweights, most
notably Alister McGrath, have already penned responses.

A very uneven collection of scriptural ridicule, amateur philosophy, historical and contemporary horror stories, anthropological speculations, and cosmological scientific arguments . . . Dawkins is operating mostly outside the range of his scientific expertise.

Thomas Nagel
Professor of Philosophy at
New York University in
The New Republic,
23rd October 2006

2

A House of Cards?

The *God Delusion* is structured rather like a house of cards. Although it purports to be 'a hard-hitting, impassioned rebuttal of religion of all types',[1] only three chapters – 2, 3 and 4 – engage with whether or not there is a God, and the remaining chapters build their increasingly angry tirades on the foundational arguments presented there. Of these three key chapters, 2 makes the hardly contentious point that people ought to have a view on the existence of God, and 3 criticises a number of arguments for belief in God, most of which you would be hard-pressed to find in Christian evangelism, biblical or contemporary.

Chapter 4, then, on Darwinian evolution, bears the load for the book as a whole, as we would expect from Dawkins' background as an evolutionary biologist, along with a number of sideswipes taken in Chapters 2 and 3. Despite its confident tone, the second half of the book

---

[1] From the jacket of the book.

simply pads out the worldview implied by the absence of a god, and does not make any substantive argument as to whether such a worldview is justified. In other words, if you strike the shepherd (Chapters 2 to 4), then the sheep (Chapters 1 and 5 to 10) will be scattered, having been rendered all-but-irrelevant. On the other hand, if the root is secure, then so are the branches.[2]

We could, only a little facetiously, characterise the structure of the book in the following table, categorising each line of argument as either A (agree), I (irrelevant), U (unsubstantiated) or D (disagree):

Ch	Section	Summary of argument and content	Comments	Category
	Preface	If there was no religion, maybe people wouldn't kill each other	Really? Cf. the 20th century	U
1	Deserved respect	Einstein did not believe in a personal God	So what?	I
	Undeserved respect	Religion should be debated the same way as anything else	Absolutely, yes it should	A
2	The God hypothesis	Yahweh killed people sometimes (cue long list of ways of saying this as emotively as possible)	Yes, he did (see section on Scripture, below)	A
	Polytheism	Some people believe in lots of gods	Yes, they do	A
		The Trinity cannot be explained properly	No, it can't	A
	Monotheism	Jews, Christians and Muslims believe in one God	Yes	A

---

[2] Matthew 26:31; Romans 11:16.

Secularism, the Founding Fathers and the religion of America	The Founding Fathers were deists or atheists, so the American religious right can't use them in support of merging church and state	Yes (but what has that got to do with God's existence?)	I
The poverty of agnosticism	Being agnostic is unsatisfactory	Yes	A
	The issue isn't proof, but probability	Yes	A
NOMA[3]	Science and religion need to be integrated	Yes	A
	Gould couldn't have meant what he said when he argued for NOMA in *Rocks of Ages*	Gould is fairly clear! In fact, Dawkins would have received a rap on the knuckles from Mrs McInerny for contesting this point[4]	U
	Miracles are empirically falsifiable	Yes (Acts 2:32)	A
The Great Prayer Experiment	Scientific studies of whether remote prayer works are a bit pathetic, and the latest one suggests it doesn't. There are good theological reasons for this	Yes (e.g. Deut 6:16; 1 Cor 1:22) – although see section on anti-supernaturalism, below	A
The Neville Chamberlain school of evolutionists	NOMA is cowardice, and people who believe in it cannot have thought it through	Maybe, but Gould, Ruse McGrath et al. are not stupid	U

[3] NOMA, which stands for 'Non-Overlapping Magisteria', is the belief that science and theism do not overlap, in terms of the way they interpret human knowledge and experience, and therefore they cannot stand in conflict to one another.

[4] The reference is from Stephen Jay Gould, 'Impeaching a Self-Appointed Judge', *Scientific American 267* (1): p. 118–121.

	Little Green Men	There might be life on other planets	So what?	I
3	Thomas Aquinas' 'proofs'	The cosmological argument does not prove a personal God	True (just read Aristotle)	A
		Omnipotent omniscience is impossible, since you cannot change your mind	Is there a six-year-old in the room? (see Num 23:19 etc.)	D
	The ontological argument and other *a priori* arguments	The ontological argument is silly	Yes (and no Christian I have ever met uses it)	A
	The argument from beauty	The existence of beauty doesn't prove the existence of God	True, but then probability is the issue, not proof	A
	The argument from personal 'experience'	The brain makes all religious experiences up. Experience tells us miracles don't happen, so if someone's experience says a miracle has happened, they are wrong	See section on anti-supernaturalism, below	D
	The argument from Scripture	The Bible is a load of rubbish, because (a) the Gospels contradict each other on where and why Jesus was born, (b) sending Joseph to Bethlehem would be like sending me to Ashby-de-la-Zouch, (c) atheists agree that it is, and so on	There is more non-sense to refute here than can fit in this box (see section on Scripture, below)	D
	The argument from admired religious scientists	Most scientists in the UK aren't Christians	Yes, but neither are most people	A
		With those that are, I remain baffled as to why they believe any of it	Irrelevant and, sadly, unsurprising	I

	Pascal's wager	Deciding to believe is impossible	Evidence?	U
		Feigning belief is obnoxious	Absolutely!	A
	Bayesian arguments	Stephen Unwin's numbers are arbitrary	Yes	A
4	The Ultimate Boeing 747	Assuming the non-eternity of God, God is more improbable than the world	What an (unstated) assumption!	U
	Natural selection as a conscious-ness-raiser	Darwin's theory of natural selection has destroyed the 'illusion' of design	Has it really? See section on the probability of God, below	D
	Irreducible complexity	God is more improbable than the world, because he is more complex	Again, assumes non-eternity	U
	The worship of gaps	Things we don't understand are not reasons to believe in God	Yes, but they can't be said to fit our theory either	A
	The anthropic principle: planetary version	The existence of life was staggeringly improbable, but it must have happened because we are here to experience it	Theism is not an alternative to the anthropic principle, but an explanation for it (as is the 'multiverse' etc).	D
	The anthropic principle: cosmological version	Our universe is staggeringly improbable, but it must have come about naturally because we are here to experience it. Any explanation is more simple than God, since God is infinitely complex	See section on the probability of God, below	D
	An interlude at Cambridge	Some religious people don't have very good reasons for their faith	Yes, sadly	A
		The nineteenth century made miracles impossible	Really? See section on anti-supernaturalism, below	D

5	The roots of religion	Given that there is no God, religious faith must have developed for a biological reason. This might be trusting your parents	There are no arguments about God's existence here	I
		Christianity probably started like the 'cargo cults' of the South Pacific	Evidence? (We have quite a lot, and it all suggests the opposite)	U
6	The roots of morality: why are we good?	Some religious people are very nasty	Yes, tragically	A
		Given that there is no God, there are other possible (evolutionary) explanations for morality	Maybe – if you grant the premiss!	U
		There are interesting moral dilemmas, which religious and irreligious people react to in the same ways	These are fascinating, but largely irrelevant to the argument	I
7	The Old Testament	People in the Old Testament did bad things	Yes (and see below)	A
		God told Abraham to sacrifice Isaac	Yes, but he knew he would intervene to be revealed as *Yahweh-yireh*	A
		Modern morality does not come from the Old Testament	Yes – and if you look at Matthew 5–7, not to mention Hebrews 8:13 etc, nor should it	A
	The New Testament	The atonement is masochistic; why couldn't God just forgive sins?	This misses the point (holiness, sin, grace) – see section on Scripture, below	D
	Love thy neighbour	Religion gives people an excuse to kill each other, although these tendencies would be there anyway	Tragically, yes (and see Matt 5:38–45)	A

	The moral *zeitgeist*	People's views about morality change	Yes (so what?)	I
	What about Hitler and Stalin? Weren't they atheists?	Stalin was, and Hitler probably wasn't, but they weren't evil because of what they believed	Having cake and eating it (cf. p. 259). Their dependence on Marx and Nietzsche's atheist arguments are obvious and frequent	U
8	Fundamentalism and the subversion of science	Unquestioning faith, based on no evidence, will conflict with legitimate scientific and historical enquiry	So will unquestioning anything (including unquestioning anti-supernaturalism!)	A
	The dark side of absolutism	We should not kill people for blasphemy	I agree (and so would Jesus, Paul, and the rest) – see e.g. Matt 7:1–5; Rom 12:18–21; Heb 10:30; etc. That does not mean these things are acceptable!	A
	Faith and homosexuality	We should not kill people (or wish death on people) for homosexuality		A
	Faith and the sanctity of human life	We should not kill people (or wish death on people) for abortion		A
	The Great Beethoven fallacy	If you believe in evolution, there is no reason to give special status to human life as opposed to other life, so abortion is fine	Once again, the premiss is the issue here	U
	How 'moderation' in faith fosters fanaticism	Moderate religion makes extremist religion possible, and therefore should be stopped at all costs	'Moderate religion' is an enemy of both extremism and atheism (e.g. Luke 9:52–55; 22:49–52)	U

9	Childhood, abuse and the escape from religion	Children should not be regarded as adherents to any faith on the basis of their parents' faith	Quite (see John 3:3–8; compare with the logic of Titus 1:6)	A
	Physical and mental abuse	*Schadenfreude* about the suffering of hell is disgraceful	Yes (and miles away from e.g. Rom 9:1–5)	A
	In defence of children	We should never indoctrinate children to the point of unquestioning adherence to anything	Yes (although there can be a fine line between indoctrination and teaching)	A
	An educational scandal	Government funding should not be given to schools that teach religion in science classes	I agree (although there are probably far more schools that teach science in religion classes. . .)	A
	Conscious-ness-raising again	Children should not be referred to as 'Christian', 'Catholic', 'Muslim', any more than 'Democrat' or 'Keynesian'	Agreed (and none in the NT are. Titus 1:6 indicates that there would be children of Christians who were not believers)	A
	Religious education as a part of literary culture	We should not throw out the Bible, because it is an important part of our literary culture	Yes, although should it not also be read historically?	A
10	Binker	God might be just a giant childhood friend, like A. A. Milne's poem about Binker	But, as Dawkins admits, belief in God persists in adulthood	U
	Consolation	Religion offers people consolation, but so might other things	Yes	I
	Inspiration	Not believing in God is inspiring to some people	Sometimes, yes	I
	The mother of all burkas	Science can be fascinating, and our understanding of the world will probably continue increasing	Yes	I

In looking at this summary, one thing should become clear, and that is just how little of the book is actually formed of arguments against God's existence. Of the 63 lines of argument (or assertion) identified above, I can happily agree with 33 (category A), many of them on biblical grounds. A further 12 are unsubstantiated (category U), either because they rest entirely on the premiss that there is no God (for instance, given that there is no God, there must be other reasons for our morality), or because they are mere assertions with no evidence offered in favour and substantial evidence against (deciding to believe in God is impossible; no one would do bad things *because* they were an atheist; Christianity probably started like a cargo cult in the South Pacific). There are then 10 which I cannot help but label irrelevant (category I), including the oft-repeated 'so-and-so did not believe in God' argument, 'the moral *zeitgeist* changes', and so on. This leaves only 8 lines, out of 63, for me to disagree with (category D), since they offer apparent reasons not to believe in God.

Now, it is only fair to say that although this schema closely follows the individual sections of the book, it is still my categorisation, not Dawkins', and I have over-simplified significantly to provide it. It should also be pointed out that the weak links do not break the chain, since theoretically it would only take one good argument to demonstrate God's non-existence. (Put less kindly, the fact that Dawkins has cluttered his book with unsubstantiated assertions, truisms and irrelevance does not, in principle, mean that his central hypothesis is wrong.)

On the other hand, the numerous sections which do not really contribute to his case clearly *do* give a sense of a greater degree of credibility, intellectual range and (often) moral superiority than is justified by the central argument itself. Dawkins says of moderate religion that it creates a context in which extremism can seem more conceivable. Ironically, the peripheral but moderate sections of the book – the vast majority of it – have exactly the same function in *The God Delusion*, creating a context in which the central but extreme thesis is made to look more plausible. When Dawkins, as all reasonable people do, condemns the horrendous behaviour of many extremists, he has not thereby made God's existence any less likely, but he can give the unguarded reader the idea that he has. As such, his quite justifiable attacks on, for instance, bombing abortion clinics or thanking God for AIDS –which incidentally would be shared by all evangelical Christians known to me personally – imply that there is an inevitable link between belief in God and appalling behaviour.

Sadly, this exemplifies the subtle but insidious fallacy of the excluded middle that recurs throughout *The God Delusion*. Christians, and by implication all religious people, are sharply divided into their two noisiest factions: fundamentalists and extreme liberals. The caricature of the former is predictably grotesque: stupid, mostly American, unquestioning and uneducated oiks who kill people for disagreeing with them, want to see Leviticus as fed-eral law, dramatise hell for twelve-year-olds, oppress women and send death-threats to eminent scientists.[5] At the opposite end of the scale, there are extreme liberals: educated people who were brought up as Christians, and then came to realise that none of the Bible is true, but continue to cling to it anyway for social or personal rea-sons.[6] The former can be rightly ridiculed for their selec-tive interpretation of Scripture and downright nastiness, the latter for their continued practice of a religion they believe to be essentially false. *Tertium non datur*.

Yet to anyone even slightly familiar with Christianity in America, let alone the UK, a very large group is miss-ing from this picture, and that is the evangelicals. There is hardly a mention in *The God Delusion* of the masses of ordinary people who believe the Bible, but do not think that gives them licence to enforce Levitical law or rejoice in gay people going to hell; no mention of the enormous group who neither abandon Scripture's authority nor believe that all of it acts as normative for today in the same way it did in the past.[7] There is certainly nothing

---

[5] Dawkins, pp. 4, 211–214, 229, 238–239, 286–298, and so on.

[6] Dawkins, pp. 147–156, 237, 335, and so on.

[7] There exist a number of hermeneutical studies at a serious, scholarly level, all of which articulate ways in which Scripture can be read as God's inspired word, without that suggesting the need take every verse and apply it uncritically, straight into our lives today. See for instance, Thiselton, *New Horizons in Hermeneu-tics* (Grand Rapids: Zondervan 1992); Wright, *The New Testament and the People of God* (London: SPCK 1992), and his shorter *The*

about the army of evangelicals who continue to start schools and hospitals; fight AIDS, slavery and exploitation rather than justify it; and campaign against injustices like child prostitution, genocide and third world debt, on the basis of their faith.[8]

Furthermore, you can hardly find a mention of any of the numerous evangelical academics who, despite Dawkins' strident allegations to the contrary, manage to combine a belief in the factual reliability of Scripture with a commitment to educational excellence, social tolerance, reasoned debate and often scientific enquiry. This is perhaps explicable – since to admit, let alone discuss, the existence of such people would considerably undermine the polemic of much of *The God Delusion* – but it surely represents a significant oversight in a book attempting to refute theism. As far as I am aware, other than the scientists (of whom more later), the only scholar who would describe himself as an evangelical mentioned in the entire book is Patrick Sookhdeo, about whose research Dawkins seems to be entirely positive,

---

Last Word (New York: HarperCollins 2005); at a popular level, Fee and Stuart, *How to Read the Bible for All Its Worth* (Grand Rapids: Zondervan 1993). At no point does Dawkins engage with these, or any others.

[8] I am confident that activists in massive Christian organisations like Tearfund and Christian Aid are just as outraged by global injustices like AIDS and slavery as Dawkins; they are certainly doing more to fight them. An excellent biblical call to campaign against injustice is given in Gary Haugen, *Good News About Injustice* (IVP: Leicester 1999).

but whose evangelicalism is, unsurprisingly, not referred to.[9] Given this remarkable series of omissions, and the frequency with which he mocks less educated believers, we could perhaps be forgiven for thinking that Dawkins has avoided picking on someone his own size.[10]

Most of the book, in fact, comprises statements, stories and sideswipes that simply do not contribute anything to the debate about whether God exists. Dawkins may not think they do either, although if he does not, it is questionable why they form such a large part of a book that is intended to persuade people out of belief in God.[11] If he does, though, we could (again, only somewhat facetiously) raise eyebrows at some of the implicit *non sequiturs*, in the manner of the website he gleefully quotes on page 85:

> ***Argument from Einstein's Unbelief:*** Einstein did not believe in a personal God. Therefore God does not exist.

> ***Argument from the Trinity:*** a three-in-one God is confusing. Therefore God does not exist.

---

[9] Dawkins, p. 307.

[10] The exception is his interaction with Swinburne, although he too is far from an evangelical. Dawkins exhibits no such reticence about quoting less intellectually qualified Christians. Despite his interviews of and disdain for fundamentalist preachers in the red states, both in print and on television, Dawkins maintains that he shies away from confrontation, since it is not well designed to get at the truth (Dawkins, p. 281). 'The lady doth protest too much, methinks.'

[11] Dawkins, p. 5.

Argument from the Founding Fathers: Thomas Jefferson and the others did not believe in a personal God, and may not have believed in a god at all. Therefore God does not exist.

Argument from Bad Arguments: There are some unconvincing and rather silly philosophical arguments for the existence of God. Therefore God does not exist.

Argument from the Ultimate Boeing 747: Given the non-existence and non-eternity of God, it is extremely unlikely that a God would have suddenly appeared from nowhere. A 'multiverse' is a simpler option. Therefore God does not exist.

Argument from Nasty Fundamentalists: Some people who believe in God use that belief to justify all sorts of terrible practices, including killing other human beings, even though Jesus told them not to. Therefore God does not exist.

Argument from Miracles: Given that miracles are impossible, miracles are impossible. So God cannot do them, and could never have done them. Therefore God does not exist.

As we have already said, none of this gentle mockery makes the central hypothesis of the book more or less true. What it does, though, is to separate the wheat from the chaff – the genuine arguments from the irrelevant, truistic or unsubstantiated. At the end of this exercise, I propose that the wheat we have left looks something like the following:

1. Omnipotent omniscience is impossible (p. 78).
2. Supernatural experiences never happen; the brain makes them up (pp. 87–92).
3. The Bible is all untrue, so we need not worry about its claims (pp. 92–97).
4. Darwin's theory of natural selection has destroyed the 'illusion' of design (pp. 114–119).
5. The existence of life is very improbable, but less improbable than God (pp. 134–141).
6. The existence of the universe is very improbable, but less improbable than God (pp. 141–151).
7. Miracles were shown to be impossible in the nineteenth century (pp. 156–157).
8. Yahweh is nasty, and the atonement masochistic (pp. 237–253).

These fall quite naturally into four categories of argument: those based on anti-supernaturalism (Chapters 2 and 7), on logic (Chapter 1), on Scripture (Chapters 3 and 8), and on improbability (Chapters 4, 5 and 6). It now remains for us to look at these categories, each in turn.

Now when they heard of the resurrection of the dead, some mocked.
But others said, 'We will hear you
again about this.'

Acts 17:32

3

Anti-supernaturalism

We start with worldview, specifically the view that the natural world we perceive with our physical senses is all there is. This anti-supernaturalist premiss on which *The God Delusion* is based – and I call it a premiss since it is frequently asserted but never argued for – simply cannot be given unquestionable status, any more than any other worldview. Although it is a common assumption that the modernist, rationalist worldview is the only one that could possibly be correct, there is no such thing as a view from nowhere, and therefore Dawkins' failure to substantiate his strident anti-supernaturalism is as potentially damaging as anyone else's failure to substantiate their theism. The space-time continuum, he assumes, is closed, brooking no intervention from a deity; therefore 'miracles' never happen by definition; therefore God does not exist. But, as he would no doubt say of theists, this argument is damagingly circular, for it assumes that which it sets out to prove. Given a materialist account of the universe, there can be no 'miracles'.[1] However, if the materialist account itself is under question – which when we are asking about the existence of God it must be – then his conclusion becomes his premiss, and vice versa.

Of course, it is well within his rights to say that he believes the possibility of 'miracles' to be immensely low based on various arguments, as he does with the existence of God in the first place. But these arguments are never put forward, unless you count the prayer experiment that even Dawkins describes as 'pathetic' (see below).[2] Furthermore, despite his lengthy protestations to the contrary, Dawkins does exhibit a remarkably nineteenth-century confidence in asserting (1) that David Hume said all there was to say about 'miracles', and (2) that the nineteenth century was 'the last time when it was possible for an educated person to admit to

---

[1] I shall continue to put the word 'miracles' in inverted commas, since what Dawkins and Hume mean by it is very different from what I mean by it. The Christian understanding of a miracle is as something which enables creation to be more fully itself, restoring the created order and redeeming it from the effects of sin. When Dawkins and Hume use the word, they seem to mean something which contravenes the created order (although they would be very unlikely to speak of the order as 'created'), in an arbitrary or random manner. The New Testament usually talks about a 'sign' (*semeion*), a 'power' or a 'mighty work' (*dunamis*), a 'wonder' (*teras*) or a 'wonderful thing' (*thaumasios*).

[2] Dawkins, pp. 61–66.

believing in miracles like the virgin birth without embarrassment'.[3] Both positions are, to say the least, open to challenge.

Hume's argument about 'miracles' was simple. A miracle can only be said to exist if the evidence for it happening is greater than the evidence against it. So far, so good. He then defines a 'miracle' as 'a violation of the laws of nature', and argues that 'as a firm and unalterable experience has established these laws, the proof against a miracle, from the very nature of the fact, is as entire as any argument from experience can possibly be imagined,' which leads him to conclude that all accounts of the miraculous are necessarily untrue.[4] Notice the syllogism:

(A) 'firm and unalterable experience' tells us that 'miracles' never happen,
(B) therefore 'miracles' never happen,
(C) therefore anyone who says that they have done is mistaken.

To this, we might well add, on behalf of Hume and Dawkins:

(D) therefore Jesus did not rise from the dead, nor was he God incarnate,

---

[3] Dawkins, p. 157; cf. p. 91.

[4] Hume, *An Enquiry Concerning Human Understanding* (New York: Collier 1909–14), 10:1.

(E) therefore Christianity is false, along with any other
    religion that believes in 'miracles'. Case closed.

From the vantage point of two hundred years later, and
in no small part thanks to a number of postmodern crit-
ics, the flaws here are fairly obvious (although not, manifestly, to Dawkins, which may explain why so many
accuse him, much to his annoyance, of being 'nineteenth century').[5] If (A) and (B) are true, then (C) to (E)
obviously follow, but it does not take Dawkins to tell us
that; the apostle Paul memorably argued it himself.[6]
What is in question is the premiss, (A), and on this point,
history suggests that experience is not perhaps as 'firm
and unalterable' as Hume believed.

   On the contrary, in fact: those who believe that nothing supernatural ever happens are in a tiny minority in
the world at large, and remain in a minority in the

---

[5] Dawkins, pp. 156–157. An alternative explanation is his
rather naïve understanding of progress, on which one review of
The God Delusion points out: 'Dawkins turns out to be an old-
fashioned Hegelian when it comes to global politics, believing in
a zeitgeist (his own term) involving ever increasing progress, with
just the occasional 'reversal' . . . [Dawkins] believes, in his Her-
bert Spencerish way, that "the progressive trend is unmistakable
and it will continue." So there we are, then: we have it from the
mouth of Mr Public Science himself that, aside from a few local,
temporary hiccups like ecological disasters, famine, ethnic wars
and nuclear wastelands, History is perpetually on the up' (Review
by Terry Eagleton in the *London Review of Books*, 19th October
2006).

[6] 1 Corinthians 15:12–14.

(relatively secular) UK.[7] No doubt Hume would have responded that this is merely a result of gullibility, credulity, misunderstood metaphor or religious bias, and in many cases this is probably true. However, to assert without qualification that it is *always* true places any account of a 'miracle' in a quite spurious Catch-22 situation: if any experience could be cited to suggest that a 'miracle' might have happened, it would (according to Hume, and Dawkins in his train) be regarded, by definition, as untrue. Heads I win, tails you lose.

Scepticism is not irreligious, of course. There are excellent reasons to believe that many alleged 'miracles' never happened, and it is just common sense to assume that the laws of nature have not been broken unless there is a good reason to believe that they have. This is true of the touching, but hardly relevant, accounts of Dawkins the child and his discovery of wind whistling through keyholes.[8] It is also very obviously true in the

---

[7] Surveys on this question continue to appear, and are usually reported on the BBC website. 72 per cent believe in a supernatural being (GfK Custom Research, 2004); 67 per cent believe in God or a higher power (ICM, 2004); 67 per cent believe in supernatural experiences (Living TV, 2002); etc. The fact that many of these people would hold contradictory views to one another, and even themselves, does not affect the main point, which is to challenge Hume's (and Dawkins') overconfidence about the 'firm and unalterable' phenomenon that is human experience. Leave the world of post-Enlightenment rationalism, for Africa or India, for instance, and the problem intensifies.

[8] Dawkins, pp. 90–91.

case of the (rather facile) straw-man example given by Dawkins of the apparition in Fatima, Portugal. Even this story, though, exposes several weaknesses in his argument.[9]

Firstly, if you refer back to the original source (a Roman Catholic website), you will find there is nothing remotely approaching evidence of 70,000 people saying they had seen the sun dance; there is, rather, evidence of 70,000 people gathered to look at the sun, eagerly expecting something remarkable due to a spreading rumour that Mary would appear to them, of whom a handful are quoted as saying they had seen exactly that. Secondly, as Dawkins notes, there are clear physical categories with which to explain what happened, including the obvious point that staring at the sun is not very good for your eyes, and would very probably result in both perceptions reported: bright colours spinning out from the sun, and a confused sense of distance.[10] Thirdly, and most importantly, the reason we (and Dawkins, if you read page 92) would obviously reject the account as historical is not that we can *a priori* rule out all 'miracles',[11] but that we have voluminous evidence that the sun did not move towards earth in the way described in 1917 (or at any other time), since the rest of the known world would have mentioned it, but did not. In other words, we have two good reasons to explain the 'apparition' in

[9] Dawkins, pp. 91–92.

[10] See the discussion of these phenomena at www.sofc.org.

[11] A priori is a Latin phrase meaning 'from first principles'.

natural terms, and more importantly, unimpeachably strong evidence that it did not happen.

Note that none of these three things can be said of the resurrection of Jesus; quite the opposite, as we shall see. Neither can they be said of a number of the healings this author has personally witnessed in the last month (September 2006). A physiotherapist friend of mine who had been wearing a wrist splint, unable to move her wrist without significant pain, was healed instantly in front of me and ten others three weeks ago, and has since been able to move it completely normally without any discomfort, much to the surprise of many of her (atheist physiotherapist) colleagues. A chef in our church, who had been unable to move his arm above shoulder level for two years, prayed for it two weeks ago during a church meeting, and was instantly able to do so (last time I looked, he had not stopped waving it for several days). A short-sighted student I know, who had never been able to walk around with no glasses without suffering migraines, was instantly healed on being prayed for, and has not worn glasses since (except when, ironically, she cautiously wore them at college, and ended up getting migraines because her eyesight had been corrected). I do not mention these examples because they are the most dramatic I know, nor are they third-hand reports in China. I mention them because I have personally witnessed them in the last few weeks, among several other 'miracles', and because they are neither internalised hallucinations nor empirically untrue, but public, physical events in the space-time world, verifiable by doctors and friends.

My point is not that anyone should become a Christian because they read these stories. All stories are open to be responded to sceptically, and these as much as any. My point is that to insist *a priori* that none of these things (and thousands like them) can possibly have happened is to fly in the face of very strong empirical evidence. It is also, crucially, to insist dogmatically on an anti-supernaturalist worldview that cannot, despite Dawkins' bluster, be assumed without debate. Every worldview has to find a way of accounting for every piece of evidence there is, whether it fits or not. And dismissing all 'miracles' as hallucinations, without any attempt to engage in debate except by quoting a few optical illusions and childhood anecdotes, is simply shouting 'liar, liar, pants on fire' with different words.

A preferable historical method is suggested in various works by the New Testament historian N. T. Wright. After the rather unquestioning dogma of Dawkins' section on 'miracles', it is refreshing to encounter the following (rather more epistemologically balanced) reflections:

> Accounts of strange happenings in any culture or tradition are of course subject to legendary accretions. But one cannot rule out *a priori* the possibility of things occurring in ways not normally expected, since to do so would be to begin from the fixed point that a particular worldview, namely the eighteenth-century rationalist one, or its

twentieth-century positivist successor, is correct in postu-
lating that the universe is simply a 'closed continuum' of
cause and effect. How can any scientific enquiry not allow
for the possibility that its own worldview might be incor-
rect? (If it is replied that certain types of argument and
enquiry would cut off the branch on which the worldview
was sitting, the counter-reply might be that, if that is where
the argument leads, you had better find yourself another
branch, or even another tree.)[12]

More thoroughgoing recent history has been coming to
the conclusion that we can only explain the evidence
before us if we reckon that Jesus did indeed perform deeds
for which there was at the time, and may well be still, no
obvious 'naturalistic' explanation – to use that terminology
for the moment . . . The church did not invent the charge
that Jesus was in league with Beelzebul; but charges like
that are not advanced unless they are needed as an explanation for some quite remarkable phenomena.[13]

Quite so. Once again, none of this is to insist that
Christianity is true because Jesus once performed 'miracles', or still performs them today. It is simply to insist
that we cannot take it as read that it isn't because he

---

[12] Wright, *The New Testament and the People of God* (London:
SPCK 1992), p. 92.

[13] Wright, *Jesus and the Victory of God* (London: SPCK 1996), pp.
186–187. The footnote accompanying the first section of this quotation cites an impressive list of those who agree, including a
number of decidedly non-Christian writers: Vermes, Meyer, Gop-
pelt, Harvey, Sanders, Borg and Crossan.

didn't. Evidence for 'miracles', in principle, should be treated like evidence for anything else.

Later on, Dawkins raises the stakes, by claiming that no educated person can 'admit to believing in miracles like the virgin birth without embarrassment' as a result of the nineteenth century.[14] This remarkable statement combines patronising modernism with sheer factual inaccuracy. Patronising modernism, because it carries the (demonstrably unhistorical) assumption that it was the nineteenth century that demonstrated the enormous improbability of 'miracles'.[15] Factual inaccuracy, in that as Dawkins himself acknowledges, there are numerous educated people who quite unashamedly believe in a whole raft of astonishing events, including the virgin birth, the resurrection of Jesus, and *ex nihilo*

---

[14] Dawkins, p. 157.

[15] For starters, we can find massive scepticism about alleged 'miracles' within the pages of the New Testament itself. The virgin birth was interpreted as a lame excuse for a child born out of wedlock (John 8:41), and Joseph sought to annul his betrothal not because he did not know where babies came from, but because he did (Matthew 1:19). The resurrection, as often reported, was met with widespread doubt (Matthew 28:17), disbelief (John 20:25; 1 Corinthians 15:12), mockery (Acts 17:32), and accusations of insanity (Acts 26:23–24). Subsequent attacks on the Christian faith focused on the resurrection as clearly ridiculous (see for example the third-century apologetic work, Against Celsus). It seems that nineteenth-century Europeans were not the first to discover that dead people stayed dead.

creation.[16] The fact that Dawkins does not believe they should is unsurprising, but it does not change the fact that they do.

The only remaining challenge to the occurrence of miracles is the account of the 'Great Prayer Experiment' of 2006, which was designed to demonstrate whether there is a correlation between prayer and events (in this case, people's physical recovery).[17] Although Dawkins concedes that the experiment was 'rather pathetic' and that Swinburne and other theologians were right to oppose it in principle, he relates the story anyway, apparently for the purpose of making fun of those who performed it.[18] Theologically, as Dawkins admits, there is a very good reason why we would *not* expect a correlation in such a test of God's power – a more biblically literate writer might point to Deuteronomy 6:16, Matthew 4:5–7, John 6:30–35 and 1 Corinthians 1:22–24 as hard evidence – but his point seems to be that the same theologians would have shown no such reticence if the

---

[16] See Dawkins, p. 99, which cites Peacocke, Stannard, Polkinghorne and Collins, and acknowledges that 'great scientists who profess religion' are 'not particularly rare'. Dawkins and his atheist colleagues may be 'baffled' as to why this is the case, but unfortunately (for them) that does not remove the problem. Quite what causes Dawkins to move the goalposts by the time of his statement on p. 157 is unclear; even if 'educated people' is taken to mean 'eminent scientists' – which would be an absurdly narrow definition – his bold pronouncement cannot stand, even on his own testimony.

[17] Dawkins, pp. 61–66.   [18] Dawkins, pp. 63–64.

survey had shown the opposite, and this is then used as a stick with which to beat them.

This is clearly speculative, and thus not a very strong argument, but it is also untrue. As it happens, the *American Heart Journal* has published several such studies between 1988 and 2006, some of which have shown a positive correlation, some a negative, and some none at all.[19] The differences between the studies are interesting, and may or may not tell us something about prayer,[20] but it is hard to find theologians who have drawn conclusions from any of them. So, at the very least, Dawkins' assumption that religious apologists would have seized on a positive result as evidence for God is questionable. Some such studies have yielded positive results, but most theologians and 'religious apologists', myself included, have been careful not to make too much of them, largely because of the Bible verses cited above.

---

[19] See the summary piece in the American Heart Journal, October 2006, Volume 152, Issue 4, pp. e41–42.

[20] The two studies which showed a positive correlation, in 1988 and 1999, had sample sizes of 393 and 990 respectively, and set the criteria for involvement as 'Born again Christians as per John 3:3 in ongoing Christian fellowship and practicing daily devotional prayer' (1988) and 'Christians with at least weekly Church attendance, daily prayer habits, and a belief in God who answers prayer and is willing and able to heal the sick' (1999). Since 2001, there have been four subsequent studies, all of which have shown virtually no correlation, with sample sizes ranging from 150 to 1802, but with far vaguer requirements, and including various religions and levels of practice. See ibid, Table 1.

Essentially, a huge amount of the argument of *The God Delusion* rests on an anti-supernaturalist premiss, and it is a premiss that is never established. We have plenty of rhetoric, but not much substance: nothing but a restatement of an oft-refuted argument of Hume's; a few anecdotes with little or no correspondence to Christian proclamation; and the (arguably justifiable) ridicule of an experiment designed to test whether prayer works or not. Trying to take out the resurrection of Jesus, miracles throughout church history and the testimonies of millions of people with arguments like these is to try and knock down the Matterhorn with a peashooter. The result is unconvincing. Suffice it to say, then, that if this is 'all that needs to be said about personal "experiences" of gods or other religious phenomena',[21] we might humbly suggest that Dawkins may be counting his chickens before they are hatched.

---

[21] Dawkins, p. 92.

Answer a fool according to his folly,
lest he be wise in his own eyes.

Proverbs 26:5

4

Logic

In this section, we can be much briefer. Some might wonder why it is worth bothering with a separate section at all, but it is entirely possible that the throwaway remark Dawkins makes about omniscient omnipotence could concern some people, and it remains a separate line of argument to the other assertions. His logic is short enough to quote in full:

> Incidentally, it has not escaped the notice of logicians that omniscience and omnipotence are mutually incompatible. If God is omniscient, he must already know how he is going to intervene to change the course of history using his omnipotence. But that means he can't change his mind about his intervention, which means he is not omnipotent.[1]

There are two responses to this rather facile argument. The first is that there is nothing new under the sun.[2] The

---

[1] Dawkins, p. 78.
[2] Ecclesiastes 1:9.

fact that omniscience means God never changes his mind, and that this poses all sorts of questions for us, is hardly something that modern logicians discovered first: Numbers 23:19 makes it crystal clear, and 1 Samuel 15:29, 35 brings the issue into sharp focus, with God being said to regret in one sense, and never to regret in another, in the space of a few verses. Clearly, it is not a new question, and nor is it one that prevented the Jews, let alone the Christians, from worshipping God.

The second is that this does not restrict omnipotence any more than the old chestnut about God creating rocks so big he cannot lift them. C. S. Lewis exposes the latter memorably:

> You may attribute miracles to him but not nonsense. This is no limit to his power . . . you have not succeeded in saying *anything* about God: meaningless combinations of words do not suddenly acquire meaning because we prefix to them the two words "God can." It remains true that all *things* are possible with God: the intrinsic impossibilities are not things but nonentities. It is no more possible for God than for the weakest of his creatures to carry out both of two mutually exclusive alternatives; not because His power meets an obstacle, but because nonsense remains nonsense even when we talk it about God.[3]

Can God do things which are logically impossible? No. Can he do things which he did not know he was going

---

[3] Lewis, The Problem of Pain in *A Mind Awake:* An Anthology of C. S. Lewis (New York: Harcourt, Brace & World 1968), p. 79.

to do? No. Can he stop being good, or holy, or glorious? No. But to infer from these things that God is not all-powerful, or (more fatuously) that God is impossible, is to build theology on a rather silly and pedantic understanding of the word 'omnipotent'. The best way to respond, perhaps, is to answer a fool according to his folly, lest he be wise in his own eyes.[4]

---

[4] Proverbs 26:5.

They received the word with all eagerness, examining the Scriptures daily to see if these things were so.

Acts 17:11

5

Scripture

We started this book with a brief look at the disdain Dawkins has for Christian theology, and suggested that this might present problems in the context of an argument about God's existence. Although this holds true throughout *The God Delusion*, it is in the sections about Scripture that it becomes most apparent. For an intelligent and educated man, Dawkins makes a surprising number of errors that do significant damage to his case. It is all very well arguing that Scripture is unreliable, but to rest that argument on a series of oversimplifications and sheer inaccuracies that most undergraduates could refute is perhaps foolhardy, and might invite the well-known riposte about eyes, specks and planks.[1] Ignorance is no more virtuous in theology than in science.

---

[1] Matthew 7:3–5.

Mad, bad or God?

Dawkins begins his section on 'the argument from Scripture' by attacking C. S. Lewis' widely-quoted argument about Jesus being 'mad, bad or God'. His approach is twofold: one, there is little evidence that Jesus thought he was divine; two, even if he did, this would not mean that he was mad, bad or God, because that trilemma ignores the 'almost too obvious' fourth possibility that Jesus was mistaken.

Whether or not we accept Lewis' argument, Dawkins' account of it actually misrepresents it. The famous passage reads:

> I am trying to prevent anyone saying the really foolish thing that people often say about Him, 'I'm ready to accept Jesus as a great moral teacher, but I don't accept His claim to be God.' That is the sort of thing we must not say. A man who was merely a man and said the sort of things Jesus said would not be a great moral teacher. He would either be a lunatic – on a level with the man who says he is a poached egg – or He would be the devil of hell. You must make a choice. Either this man was, and is, the Son of God, or else a madman or something worse. You can shut Him up for a fool, you can spit at Him and kill Him as a demon, or you can fall at His feet and call Him Lord and God. But let us not come up with any patronising nonsense about His being a great human teacher. He has not left that open to us. He did not intend to.[2]

---

[2] Lewis, *Mere Christianity*, (New York: Macmillan 1952), pp. 55–56.

All other things being equal, the statement 'I am x' could be true, or false. If false, it could be deliberately false (a lie), or accidentally false, and if accidentally false, it could be the product of insanity, or of a reasonable mind. Dawkins accuses Lewis of omitting to mention the final possibility, that Jesus was honestly mistaken. This would be fine if 'I am x' had been a statement like 'I am a good chess player' – it would not necessarily mean I was insane if it turned out I was wrong, because I could have been mistaken. But imagine 'I am x' was something like 'I am the light of the world', or 'Before Abraham was, I am', or 'I am the bread that came down from heaven', or 'I and the Father are one'.[3] In that sort of situation, the 'reasonable mind' option becomes virtually unthinkable.

And this is what Lewis points out in the above passage: that anyone who was mistaken *about the sorts of things Jesus said* would be, effectively, mad. I am unsure whether Dawkins' statement that 'plenty of people are' honestly mistaken like this refers to being mistaken in general (in which case his comment is irrelevant), or being mistaken about being divine (in which case his comment is unsubstantiated and surely untrue – I am unaware of any reasonably minded individuals in the world who believe themselves to be God, and Dawkins does not mention any). But if Jesus did say things like this, then Lewis is surely right: he must have been

---

[3] John 8:12; 8:58; 6:41; 10:30.

deliberately misleading people, or mentally unsound, or God. The real debate, then, is whether Jesus actually did say things like this. The document we call John's Gospel says that he did. Dawkins (obviously) believes that he did not, since 'there is no good historical evidence'.[4] Without being certain what presuppositions this sentence contains – it may be that Dawkins' definition of 'good historical evidence' excludes such a conclusion *a priori* – it is presumably clear that if Jesus did, say these things then Lewis' argument is actually very strong.

The historical reliability of the Gospels

Dawkins then moves on to the major plank of his argument, which is that the Gospels are unreliable sources, and therefore they should not be used to substantiate belief in God. A number of things are strange about this section of his book, not least the easily avoidable mistakes it contains, but perhaps the strangest is that it does not attack the right target at all. Very little Christian preaching, in the first or twenty-first centuries, has depended on the stories of inns, stars, shepherds and wise men in the opening chapters of Matthew and Luke. The New Testament provides support for believing in God in that (a) it is a compilation of 27 separate documents from various authors throughout the first century of Christian belief, which both argue for and depend on

---

[4] Dawkins, p. 92.

the historical fact of Jesus' resurrection, and (b) these documents depict the various ways in which the early disciples came to terms with what had happened, including their gradual realisation that Jesus was God himself. To be fair, you would not appreciate this from reading *The God Delusion*, and it may be that Dawkins does not see it either (which would perhaps explain his failure to engage with it). But to limit his engagement with Scripture to the first two chapters of Matthew and Luke, as Dawkins essentially does, is intellectually irresponsible.[5]

We have mentioned the various problems, errors and oversimplifications in this section a few times now, so it is probably worth listing them, since they pose huge problems for Dawkins' presentation. In the order in which they appear:

Were the New Testament writers unbiased observers?

Once again, the spectre of nineteenth-century modernism and twentieth-century positivism casts its shadow over the argument. Of course the New Testament writers were not unbiased observers. Neither are any other writers, then or now. And certainly, no one

---

[5] Dawkins, pp. 93–95. Although I disagree with them, there are plenty of believers who have questions or doubts about some of the historical details in Matthew 1–2 and Luke 1–3. This does not mean they are right, but it does mean that merely listing these questions is insufficient.

could possibly be 'unbiased' about anything as significant as whether or not the God of Israel had just raised Jesus from the dead. Neutrality on questions like this is impossible, because as soon as a writer expresses faith or scepticism, they have immediately taken sides. The fact is, we have over 20 documents – the majority of which were written by people *who were not disciples at the time of the resurrection* – which document the resurrection, its consequences, and the community that resulted. We have no such documents arguing the opposite, biased or otherwise.

Paul's letters mention almost none of the 'facts' of Jesus' life

Paul certainly does not give many details of Jesus' life in his letters, although 'almost none' is an exaggeration.[6] But regarding the big 'fact', the resurrection, which Dawkins would presumably see as the most unlikely component of the Gospel accounts, Paul says an awful lot.[7] Arguing that he has nothing to say about the reliability or otherwise of the Gospels is thus a bit misleading.

Many generations of scribal 'Chinese Whispers'

The 'Chinese Whispers' argument used to be commonplace. It was widely assumed that the scribes were

---

[6] 1 Corinthians 7:10–11; 11:23–26; 15:3–7; etc.

[7] There are so many references to the resurrection in Paul that it would be flogging a dead horse to quote them all, but the classic passage, 1 Corinthians 15, is the fullest treatment.

frequently inaccurate in their copying of Scriptural texts, and that it was therefore impossible to find what the originals had actually said. With the discovery of the Dead Sea Scrolls in 1947, however, it became clear that the copying of the scribes was astonishingly accurate, and that a minimal number of changes had occurred in the text of the Old Testament between the first and tenth centuries AD (and those that had occurred were inconsequential).[8] In other words, over a thousand years of copying, the text remained almost exactly the same, and therefore the 'Chinese Whispers' theory is demonstrably misleading.

Matthew, Luke and John contradict each other about Jesus' birth

Given the amount that has been written about the birth of Jesus in the Gospels, the mistakes in this section are somewhat surprising. In essence, Dawkins presents his evidence for 'glaring contradictions' as follows: (1) when the Gospels were written, no one knew where he was born; (2) John says Jesus' followers were surprised that he was not born in Bethlehem; (3) Matthew says Mary

---

[8] The Dead Sea Scrolls date from, at the latest, the first century AD, whereas the earliest extant copies of the Old Testament we have are from the ninth and tenth centuries AD. In that thousand-year period, almost nothing in the text had changed. Possibly it is Dawkins, rather than the scribes, who has a case of 'colouring by religious agendas' (Dawkins, p. 93).

and Joseph were in Bethlehem all along; (4) Luke says they went there because of a census, having previously lived in Nazareth. Three of these four statements are simply false. (1) Two of the four Gospels say where Jesus was born, and they both agree it was Bethlehem. The assertion that 'no one knew', and that the evangelists therefore made it up, is building castles in the air, with no supporting evidence. (2) John 7:41–44 says nothing about 'his followers' querying his birthplace. Far from it: the Jewish people at the Feast of Tabernacles were divided about him, with some thinking him the Christ and/or the Prophet and following him, and others thinking he couldn't be since he did not come from Bethlehem, and therefore wanting to kill him.[9] (3) Matthew does not say that Mary and Joseph were there all along. He does not comment at all on where they lived prior to the birth of Jesus, not even mentioning geography until his announcement of Jesus' birth in Matthew 2:1. (4) This last point is correct, but obviously in itself provides no evidence for a contradiction. The likely explanation, which in Dawkins' terms is 'almost too obvious to need mentioning',[10] is that Joseph and Mary lived in Nazareth, went to Bethlehem for Jesus' birth, and

---

[9] Nathanael, of course, does query the provenance of Jesus (John 1:46), but this does not mention Bethlehem, and has nothing whatever to do with the dialogue in John 7 quoted by Dawkins.

[10] Dawkins, p. 92, on what he regards as C. S. Lewis' false trilemma of 'mad, bad or God'

returned to Nazareth soon afterwards to raise him, which resulted in the common perception that he had been born there, and not in Bethlehem. This is how Luke describes it, and it in no way presents 'glaring contradictions' with the accounts of Matthew or John.[11]

The Romans sending Joseph to the town of Bethlehem is complete nonsense

The argument here, which Dawkins credits to A. N. Wilson and Robin Lane Fox, is that the Romans would never have sent Joseph to the city where 'a remote ancestor had lived a millennium earlier' – it would be like sending Dawkins back to Ashby-de-la-Zouch as a result of his Norman ancestry. It is tempting to suggest that if Dawkins had read some New Testament scholars on this issue, he might have avoided making such an odd claim, with its even odder (although very amusing) comparison.[12] To describe David as 'a remote ancestor' is

---

[11] One might as well accuse Dawkins of contradicting himself for referring to the sun tearing itself from the heavens in one place (p. 91), but dancing in another (p. 92). A contradiction is to say that both 'A' and 'not A' are true, not to say that both 'A' and 'B' are true.

[12] I am aware of the intellectual snobbery that is implied by this sentence, and obviously there is nothing wrong with those who are not New Testament scholars debating the relevant passages. But there is a parallel between the arguments of someone like Wilson and those of Michael Behe which Dawkins rubbishes in Chapter 4, and the dismissal of Wilson in scholarly books like

extraordinary. Anyone familiar with Judaism would be well aware both that tribal lineage was a crucial part of a Jew's self-understanding, as in some cases it still is, and that descent from David, the definitive king in the tribe of Judah, would have been a cherished part of an individual's identity. When your family history, land, property, marriage rights and inheritance all depend on who you descend from, nothing is more natural than recording your ancestry, particularly those ancestors who were especially distinguished or anointed (which explains the need for the otherwise tedious opening chapters of 1 Chronicles, not to mention of Matthew's Gospel as well). In contemporary terms, therefore, the parallel is not with going back to Ashby-de-la-Zouch where your Norman forebears came from, but with recording your place of birth, citizenship and mother's maiden name: descent from David, and hence Judah, showed who you were and where you came from. Dawkins' mockery of this idea, frankly, shows an ignorance of first-century Judaism.[13]

N. T. Wright, *Jesus and the Victory of God* (London: SPCK 1996) is even briefer than, although nothing like as scathing as, the dismissal of Behe in Dawkins, pp. 125–134. In this instance, Dawkins' reliance on books you can buy in Waterstone's bookshop leads him astray on important historical issues.

[13] I remember making a fool of myself a few years ago, when I asked a friend of mine where her surname, Levy, came from. She stared at me for a while before remarking that, of all people, I should know where it came from, and that it could lay claim to being the oldest surname in the world. Tribes matter.

The conflict with Josephus

Here, Dawkins is right on one thing: Josephus does not mention the census to which Luke refers. But his conclusion, that Luke has got it wrong on matters of history, is again misleading. Several alternatives have been offered by scholars, including the possibility that the Greek word *protos* should be understood as 'before' rather than 'first',[14] but even if Luke and Josephus disagreed, it would not prove that Luke was wrong (since there is no third source available to tip the weight of probability for one side or the other), and it certainly would not constitute a contradiction within Scripture. The last two hundred years have seen a number of allegations of incompetence levelled at Luke by sceptics, including several which have been subsequently and sheepishly retracted in the light of fresh evidence. Had Dawkins been writing in the nineteenth century, he would have been crowing that Luke was a fool because he thought the rulers in Thessalonika were called *politarches*, or that Lysanias was the tetrarch of Abilene in AD 27, details which have since been verified archaeologically.[15] Similarly, the accuracy of Luke's descriptions of traditions, rulers, dates, buildings and seafaring in the first century should make us very wary of assuming he is wrong about the census.

---

[14] Raymond Brown's massive *The Birth of the Messiah* (New York: Doubleday 1979) goes into some length on this question and others surrounding the birth narratives.

[15] Acts 17:8; Luke 3:1.

Many contradictions between Matthew and Luke

This section is very peculiar. Dawkins quotes two atheist journalists, neither of whom seems to have any training in biblical studies or theology (one is a sociologist and the other an anthropologist), as having demonstrated contradictions between Matthew and Luke. According to one, Matthew is so keen to fulfil messianic prophecies that he describes Jesus' 'descent from David, birth in Bethlehem' – but then so does Luke, in 1:32 and 2:1 respectively. On the other hand, Luke wants the Gentiles to be in on things, so he presses 'the hot buttons of pagan Hellenistic religions (virgin birth, veneration by kings, etc.)' – which is strange, since Matthew also describes the virgin birth (1:18–21), and venerating kings are nowhere in sight in any of the accounts (although they do have a starring role in a famous Christmas carol, which may explain their appearance here). Worst of all, it is Matthew, not Luke, who describes the visit of the Magi (Matthew 2:1–12), which completely undermines the Hellenistic button-pushing theory Dawkins is proposing. One cannot but wonder whether Dawkins has even read the narratives about which he is so dismissive. Likewise the genealogies, while superficially more confusing, do not cancel each other out at all, although Matthew has certainly been theologically motivated in his selection.[16] At any rate, this entire section of Dawkins' book is full of errors.

---

[16] See, among others, Leon Morris, *Matthew*, PNTC (Grand

The arbitrary choice of the four canonical Gospels

We have already commented on Dawkins' amusing statement that Jefferson was referring to as-yet-undiscovered 'Gospels' in a letter to his nephew. The essence of his point here, though, seems to be that there were a number of 'Gospels' which could have been put in the Bible, but weren't, and that this process was 'arbitrary'. Quite apart from his failure to engage with how the canon of Scripture evolved, and his unquestioning trust in Bart Ehrman's version of things, the main problem here is that there are excellent historical reasons to believe that the canonical Gospels are both chronologically nearer to, and historically more reliable about, the events concerning Jesus than documents like the *Gospel of Thomas*.[17] Dawkins, perhaps speaking better than he knows, writes that the Gnostic Gospels include 'embarrassingly implausible' stories, and he is right. The canonical Gospels, as a brief glance indicates, are totally different sorts of documents from *Thomas* and the rest, containing narrative, historical dates and facts that can be checked, and a heavily Jewish flavour, which is exactly what we would expect if they were writing history about a Jewish prophet. To lump them all together as 'legends' like those of King Arthur is thus absurd.[18]

Rapids: Eerdmans 1992); Joel Green, *The Gospel According to Luke*, NICNT (Grand Rapids: Eerdmans 1997).

[17] See, for instance, N. T. Wright, *The New Testament and the People of God* (London: SPCK 1992), Chapters 13 and 14.

[18] 'In the fifteenth year of the reign of Tiberius Caesar, Pontius

The 'common source'

Of all the unsubstantiated points made in *The God Delusion*, this is perhaps the hardest to trace. It is unclear to me where Dawkins has got the idea from that all the Gospels share one common source (which would be quite a biblical-critical bombshell for sceptics and believers alike), let alone that this one source might have been 'a lost work of which Mark is the earliest extant document', so it is hard to know how to respond. The simplest way is maybe to state that current scholarly opinion, both evangelical and sceptical, holds that Matthew and Luke are largely derived from two sources, Mark and 'Q', with two other sources, known as 'M' and 'L', accounting for their unique material. I have yet to encounter any New Testament scholar who believes that John was derived from Mark, and I doubt I ever will.

Now, some blunders like this are understandable from an armchair enthusiast. But from someone writing against the historicity of the Gospels and the 'delusion' of belief in God, and from someone who (rightly) gets cross with his opponents for making simple mistakes,

---

Pilate being governor of Judea, and Herod being tetrarch of Galilee, and his brother Philip tetrarch of the region of Ituraea and Trachonitis, and Lysanias tetrarch of Abilene, during the high priesthood of Annas and Caiaphas, the word of God came to John the son of Zechariah in the wilderness' (Luke 3:1–2). Sentences like that are commonplace in works of history, but impossible to find in King Arthur, Thomas, The Gospel of Philip, The Gospel of Mary Magdalen, or for that matter the Qur'an.

they are quite inexcusable. In the space of six pages, Dawkins has built his case for the unreliability of the Bible on a string of oversimplifications and errors, and by the time he cites G. A. Wells, an emeritus professor of German, as saying that Jesus might not have existed, his credibility has been badly eroded. If we are looking for 'gaping holes', they will be more easily found in *The God Delusion* than in the canonical Gospels.

The elephant in the room

All of the above, though relevant, does not strike at the main point. The main point is that Dawkins has the relationship between Scripture and mainstream Christian belief completely upside-down. The assumption underlying almost all that Dawkins says about the Bible is that Christians structure their beliefs as follows:

(A) the Bible is all true, and
(B) the Bible says Jesus rose from the dead and is God incarnate.

Therefore

(C) Jesus rose from the dead, and
(D) Jesus is God incarnate.

Now, even if this was what Christians believed, we have just seen that Dawkins' challenge to (A) is woefully inadequate. But this is not, in the main, what Christians, and certainly evangelicals, believe. The evangelical structure of belief, as articulated by a plethora of writers from Paul to the present,[19] is:

(A) the historical evidence within and without Scripture points to the fact that Jesus rose from the dead.

Therefore

(B) Jesus rose from the dead, which

(C) showed that he was vindicated by God and was Lord of the world;

and therefore

(D) we should treat the things he said and did, and the things his apostles said and did, as authoritative.

The authority, and accuracy, of Scripture is thus a conclusion, not a starting point, for evangelicals. The starting point is that the historical evidence, both inside and outside the Bible, points to the fact that Jesus rose from the dead.

The arguments have been made so well and so simply elsewhere that it is only needed to restate them here. We certainly start from an empty tomb; even non-Christian historical scholars admit as much.[20] We can be sure of

---

[19] So, Romans 1:1–6. A wonderfully brief and lucid example is given in John Piper, *Desiring God* (Portland: Multnomah 1986), pp. 239–250. This way round of thinking is also well expressed and argued for at a scholarly level in the various works of N. T. Wright, particularly his outstanding *The Resurrection of the Son of God* (London: SPCK 2002).

[20] Geza Vermes, *Jesus the Jew:* A Historian's Reading of the

this for three main reasons. Firstly, if the tomb was not empty, then the Christian movement would have been instantly scuppered just by someone going and getting the body. Secondly, the Christian story about the bribe to the soldiers (Matthew 28:11–15) would only have been needed if there was a story about soldiers falling asleep, which in turn would only have been needed if the tomb was actually empty and people needed to find a way to explain it. Thirdly, the Christians made the empty tomb central to their early preaching, which would have been a very silly move unless people knew it was true. The empty tomb is as secure a historical fact as we are likely to find.

There are four main theories to explain how the tomb became empty, two of which can be ruled out from the start. (1) The authorities, whether Jewish or Roman, stole Jesus' body, and the disciples mistakenly assumed he had been raised, inventing stories of appearances afterwards. The reason this is so clearly wrong is that both the Jewish and Roman authorities were, within a short period of time, trying to stop the Christian movement from growing, and if they had stolen his body they

Gospels (London: Collins 1973), p. 41: 'When every argument has been considered and weighed, the only conclusion acceptable to the historian must be that the opinions of the orthodox, the liberal sympathizer and the critical agnostic alike – and even perhaps of the disciples themselves – are simply interpretations of the one disconcerting fact: namely that the women who set out to pay their last respects to Jesus found to their consternation, not a body, but an empty tomb.'

would simply have produced it. (2) Jesus did not really die, but fell into some sort of unconscious state, then revived in the tomb, and moved the stone himself. This is even more ridiculous, if you know anything about Roman crucifixion. Soldiers executed hundreds of people a year, they knew exactly what they were doing, and no one could survive it, far less roll away a two-ton stone and then take out two guards:

> . . . it is noticeable that even those historians who are passionately committed to denying the resurrection do not attempt to go by this route . . . The only other thing worth pointing out about this theory is its remarkable self-reference: though frequently given the *coup de grace*, it keeps reviving itself – carrying about as much conviction as a battered but revived Jesus would have done.[21]

(3) The disciples stole the body, and then (a) imagined or (b) pretended that they had seen him alive afterwards. If people are going to say Jesus did not rise from the dead, this is the best option they have. But consider it for a moment. (a) The number of independent and yet near-identical hallucinations that would have been needed to generate the early church's proclamation is totally unbelievable, and without even close parallel.[22] The ancient world knew dead people didn't rise; like us, they knew

---

[21] Wright, *Resurrection* (London: SPCK 2002), p. 709.

[22] I have commented above on the example Dawkins uses from Fatima in 1917. The more widely cited example is the study of Leon Festinger, on which see Wright, *Resurrection*, pp. 697–701.

that if they had a vision of someone who had died recently, that did not prove that they were alive, but dead. And if the disciples had taken the body, it would be utterly incredible that they would then all have had the same hallucination without anyone remembering they had stolen it themselves. The most obvious problem with (b) is that many of the witnesses were killed and tortured for their proclamation of Jesus' resurrection, which you would be very unlikely to undergo if you had made it up. Of course, people today are martyred for all sorts of strange ideas, but there is a big difference: right-minded people may die for things they can't prove are true, but they won't die for things they *can* prove are *not* true. (This is even clearer when you are dealing with unbelieving sceptics, which is certainly what Paul, and James the brother of Jesus, were.) Then you've got the women finding the body – as much as we don't like it, women were just not acceptable as witnesses to first-century Jews, so if you were to invent a story about an empty tomb you would never have women being the ones to find it. Worst of all, the sources we have are unanimous that the disciples were definitely *not* expecting Jesus to rise from the dead. Option (3) simply does not stack up.

Which only leaves option (4): that God raised Jesus from the dead. Notice that the argument used has not assumed that there is a God – the word wasn't even mentioned – but rather, it has just not assumed that there isn't (which, perhaps, is the main difference between the Christian and the sceptic at this point). This is to say, as a historical conclusion, that there is only one plausible explanation of the empty tomb, let alone the numerous resurrection appearances we know about. And this means that the resurrection actually happened.

As has already been commented, Dawkins never engages with the resurrection, and there may be various reasons for this. But in a book purporting to undermine belief in God, and certainly in the Christian God, it is a massive problem. From the earliest days of the church, the resurrection was central to Christian belief and practice. To make fun of the ontological argument while ignoring the resurrection, and to think that one has thereby removed the basis for belief in God, is to chase the mice out of the sitting-room, and thus announce that the house is free of animals, while there is an elephant grinning on the sofa.

Scripture and the character of God

The final category of biblical argument is more polemic, and therefore can be responded to more quickly. It was characterised earlier as 'Yahweh is nasty, and the atonement masochistic'. Given what we have seen of Dawkins' view of, and understanding of, Scripture, it would not be totally surprising to discover that he had misunderstood the character of God and his plan of salvation. And this is exactly what we do find; sometimes obviously, as when he implies that God approved of the

terrible behaviour in the book of Judges,[23] and sometimes more subtly, as when he insinuates that God's jealousy for Israel is tantamount to a toddler tantrum, or
that believing man's sin is worth God bothering about –
let alone crushing his Son for – simply reflects human
egocentricity.[24] I have written about these issues, including the character, holiness and love of God, and the
wonder of the atonement, elsewhere.[25] But for the
moment, suffice it to say two things: that Dawkins, once
again, has made several mistakes in his presentation;[26]

---

[23] For example, Jephthah's rash vow (Judges 11:1–40), and the
story of the Levite and the concubine (Judges 19:1–30); see
Dawkins, pp. 240–243. The disapproval of Yahweh at these
events and numerous others like them is clearly indicated by the
phrase 'everyone did what was right in his own eyes' (Judges
17:6; 21:25; cf. Deuteronomy 12:8).

[24] This version of things misses most major Judeo-Christian
themes, including man in the image of God (which explains God's
interest in our species); sin as defacing that image (which explains
the severity of the problem and the need for a solution); holiness
(which accounts for God's justice needing to be satisfied by
Christ); and the exclusive nature of God's love for his people
(which accounts for his jealousy). It is not surprising, then, that
the resulting analysis is so confused.

[25] Andrew Wilson, *Incomparable:* Exploring the Character of
God (Eastbourne: Survivor Books [Kingsway], forthcoming in
June 2007).

[26] The attribution of Hebrews to the apostle Paul, on the
authority of Geza Vermes is very strange; the last scholarly
defence of Pauline authorship, now almost universally rejected,
was that of William Leonard in 1939 (see Leonard, *The Authorship
of the Epistle to the Hebrews:* Critical Problem and Use of the Old

and that even if he had not, his section on the character of God would not show that such a God does not exist, merely that Dawkins does not like him. To be fair, all that Dawkins is seeking to show in these sections is that we do not derive our morality from the Bible. But under the surface is the idea that we *should* not, and this can be robustly refuted with a more measured reading of Scripture. It is certainly no reason not to believe in God.

Testament [Rome: Vatican Polygot Press 1939]). In a different vein, arguing that 'love thy neighbour' in the New Testament is only intended to apply to Jews is to utterly miss the point of that wonderful parable of the good Samaritan (Luke 10:25–37).

Lift up your eyes on high and see: who created these?

Isaiah 40:26

6

Improbability

As we would expect, given his background, Dawkins rests a huge amount of weight on his fourth chapter, which is confidently entitled, 'Why there almost certainly is no God'. Admirably, this chapter is very clearly laid out, so it is very straightforward for a layperson to understand. It essentially comprises three points:

(1) God is the most improbable being that could exist, since he is so complex;

(2) Darwininan evolution has destroyed the 'illusion' of design, since there is no such thing as irreducible complexity, and any creature that is complex is still significantly simpler than any god figure;

(3) the anthropic principle provides an alternative to design or creation – the existence of matter, life, the eucaryotic cell and consciousness are exceptionally improbable but, again, less improbable than the 'God

hypothesis', and there are various other ways of explaining them.

It should be noted from the outset that there are many evolutionary biologists who strongly believe in the God of the Bible as revealed in Jesus of Nazareth, and that therefore the leap from natural selection to confident atheism is a massive and unnecessary one.[1] However, these three arguments may be seen to hold water in and of themselves, and we shall therefore look at each of them in turn.

The Ultimate Boeing 747

Dawkins begins this chapter with characteristic clarity: 'The argument from improbability is the big one.'[2] Such statements are commonly used by theists, jeering at the confidence materialists place in a string of almost unthinkably improbable coincidences, but to Dawkins, 'the argument from improbability, properly deployed, comes close to proving that God does *not* exist'. Taking

---

[1] Such thinkers are common, but the most accessible explanations of this belief are presented in John Polkinghorne, *Science and Christian Belief:* Theological Reflections of a Bottom-Up Thinker (London: SPCK 1994); more recently, Francis Collins, *The Language of God* (New York: Free Press 2006). See also the various works of Alister McGrath, including his *Dawkins' God:* Genes, Memes and the Meaning of Life (Malden: Blackwell 2004).

[2] Dawkins, p. 113.

his terminology from the astronomer Fred Hoyle, he then describes his basis for saying that God, not the existence of life from non-life, is the most improbable thing there is, calling him or it the Ultimate Boeing 747.[3] This then becomes the basis for his preference for any other explanations, which include, as we shall see, some fairly odd ones. Life out of non-life may be improbable, he argues, but nothing is as improbable as God.

The problem with all this is fairly fundamental, and amounts to an unstated premiss which appears no less than twelve times in Chapter 4. Given the non-eternity of God, the appearance of an infinitely complex deity is, of course, massively improbable. If we could establish that, quadrillions of years ago, there was no divine being in existence, then positing the creation of God, and his subsequent creation of the universe, would be absurdly improbable.[4] But this is not what any theist I have come across believes, since the Christian God is, by definition, uncreated, infinite, and everlasting. This argument is also explicitly overturned by the very first phrase of the Bible: 'In the beginning, God . . .' Dawkins, of course,

---

[3] Hoyle's analogy was that the chance of getting life out of non-living matter was the equivalent of getting a Boeing 747 from the materials strewn about a junkyard.

[4] This is all that is established by arguments like the following, which pop up several times in this chapter: '. . . the designer himself (/herself/itself) immediately raises the problem of his own origin. Any entity capable of designing something as improbably as a Dutchman's Pipe (or a universe) would have to be even more improbable than a Dutchman's Pipe' (Dawkins, p. 120).

does not believe in an eternal God, and may not believe that we could ever establish his likelihood. But he cannot use the contingency and non-eternity of God as a basis for arguing that God is improbable. A contingent, created, non-eternal god would be the Ultimate Boeing 747. An eternal God who had always existed would not.

So, a non-eternal god is immensely unlikely. What of an eternal God? Given that we cannot go back quadrillions of years to see how it all began, and that any arguments advanced in favour of God's likelihood or otherwise will depend at some point on his eternal existence or eternal non-existence, how could we proceed? The answer is, of course, the same as it is for any belief, religious or otherwise: we look at the information we have available, form a hypothesis, see how the data fits with that hypothesis, and adjust it accordingly. And, in this case, one important piece of data relates to the nature of the world around us. If there was an eternal and omnipotent God, the world as it is would not be particularly improbable – an eternal and omnipotent God would have no problem creating it. If there was not, then the world as it is would be spectacularly improbable, as Dawkins (grudgingly) allows.[5]

None of this proves God, of course. It simply shows that the Ultimate Boeing 747 line of argument is based

---

[5] Unless, that is, you are allowed the luxury of inventing billions of other universes to increase the odds. That this rather silly speculation is so often the last line of defence offered by atheists seems to me a telling point against them; see below.

on a mistaken premiss, and that Dawkins' subsequent invocation of it is to be questioned.

Irreducible complexity and the illusion of design

This section builds on the previous one. Natural selection, Dawkins argues, provides a clear explanation for the development of complex life forms without recourse to a designer. Irreducible complexity, he contends, is a myth, a piece of intellectual laziness dreamt up to stop scientists finding out what really happened. And the fact that natural selection can replace design in biology should give us confidence that, if we just wait long enough, an explanation may be found that can replace design in the emergence of life, cells and consciousness. Therefore there is no need for the Ultimate Boeing 747, God.

It would be possible, as many do, to begin a lengthy battle with Dawkins about whether natural selection or intelligent design is the best explanation of the development of complex life, given the existence of simple living organisms. We are not going to do this here, not because it is unimportant (clearly it is very important), but because it is largely irrelevant to the case Dawkins makes – both educated Christians and educated non-Christians can be found on both sides, and as such, evolution by natural selection is no evidence for or against God's existence.[6] A few comments will suffice.

---

[6] Both agnostics and evangelical Christians have taken both sides of the debate. Amongst non-Christians, see particularly

It is not clear that Dawkins' tirade against the concept of irreducible complexity is entirely fair. To be sure, there have been many who have seized on 'gaps' as evidence, only to be confounded years later, but as Dawkins knows, it is often Christians who have protested against this approach.[7] On the other hand, there are a number of examples that could potentially display a complexity which, while not provably irreducible, nevertheless do not fit well with our current understanding, to say no more for the present. When faced with these – my personal favourite is the bombardier beetle[8] – Dawkins is right to say that each developmental stage cannot be asserted *not* to be advantageous without further argument or justification. But it could equally be said that to assert that each stage *is* advantageous without justification, as he appears to do in this instance, is equally unsatisfactory. Obviously, he would expect us to give

Philip Johnson's *Darwin on Trial* (Downers Grove: IVP 1991) on intelligent design, or Dawkins' own *The Blind Watchmaker* (New York: Norton 1986) on natural selection. Amongst evangelicals, there are many more advocates of special creation (Lee Strobel's *The Case for a Creator* summarises many of these), but there remain a number of those who believe evolution by natural selection and ex nihilo creation by God are easily compatible: see for instance Kenneth Miller, *Finding Darwin's God* (New York: HarperCollins 1999); Collins, *The Language of God;* and the overview in McGrath, *The Twilight of Atheism*, pp. 79–111.

[7] Dawkins, p. 125, on Bonhoeffer; p. 131, on Kenneth Miller.

[8] The bombardier beetle has a very unusual defence mechanism. It has tubes in its tail which store two different chemicals, and these chemicals, when mixed together, cause an explosion. It

natural selection the benefit of the doubt, as many do. But to use this argument to torpedo any potential examples of irreducible complexity may not be allowing the evidence to point where it leads.

The same is true in the rather more everyday examples he quotes like eyes and wings, where he may be guilty of a bit of misdirection. Discussing wings, he writes:

> Half a wing could save your life by easing your fall from a tree of a certain height. And 51 per cent of a wing could save you if you fall from a slightly taller tree. Whatever fraction of a wing you have, there is a fall from which it will save your life where a slightly smaller winglet would not . . . the forests are replete with examples with gliding or parachuting animals illustrating, in practice, every step . . .[9]

This is slightly misleading. It implies that irreducible complexity founders on the difference between a larger wing and a 'slightly smaller winglet', but that is not the point of those who say a wing is irreducibly complex. (Not being a biologist, I am unable to pronounce on it

---

also has a third substance, an inhibitor, which prevents any explosion from taking place until the chemicals enter a chamber in its rear; at this point an enzyme is added and an explosion takes place, firing a 100°C jet out of its backside at its enemies, and propelling itself several feet away. It is not clear how natural selection, which requires each step to be advantageous, could ever have produced a bombardier beetle that did not immediately blow itself to smithereens.

[9] Dawkins, pp. 123–124.

either way.) Their argument is that the development of the wing in the first place is the issue, not its subsequent increase in size. In that sense, for a bird to have 51 per cent of a wing would not mean having a developed wing half the size, but to have some bones, muscles and feathers in place and not others. Dawkins obviously knows this, but his language suggests that size is the issue, and while there are plenty of creatures in the forests with small wings, it is not clear that there are any who have wing bones without wing muscles, or some wing bones without others. As such, his statement that 'the forest is replete' with examples of 'every step' is surely an exaggeration, and his section on wings could give the unguarded reader the impression that irreducible complexity is far less tenable than it actually is.

Likewise, the thorny question is not how the wings got bigger, but how the independent stages all needed for wing development in the first place – bone growth, feather coating, muscular adaptation – all happened at the same time: the difference between 0 per cent and 10 per cent of a wing, rather than 50 per cent and 60 per cent, if you will. I am unsure how ironic he was being in his closing comments, but the following interview with Dawkins by Jonathan Miller draws attention to the difficulty of assuming each developmental stage must have been advantageous in itself:

Miller: Something has to explain the novelties themselves.

Dawkins: Well, the novelties themselves, of course, are genetic variations in the gene pool which ultimately come from mutation and more proximately come from sexual re-combination. There's nothing very inventive or ingenious about these novelties, I mean they are random. And they mostly are deleterious – most mutations are bad. So you really need to focus on natural selection as the positive side and it's only natural selection that produces living things, which have the illusion of design. The illusion of design does not come from the novelty.

Miller: What was it about that early novelty, before it culminated in something as useful as a feather? Where could natural selection get its purchase upon something which was no more than a pimple?

Dawkins: There cannot have been intermediate stages which were not beneficial. There's no room in natural selection for the sort of, um, foresight argument, that says 'Well, we've got to let it persist for the next million years and it'll start becoming useful.' That doesn't work. There's got to be a selection pressure all the way.

Miller: So there isn't a process, as it were, going on in the cell saying, 'Look, be patient . . .'

Dawkins: No . . .

Miller: '. . . it's going to be a feather, believe me! Yes, that's right, yes . . .'

Dawkins: It doesn't happen like that. There's got to be a series of advantages all the way in the feather. If you can't think of one, then that's your problem, not natural selection's problem. Natural selection – well, I suppose that is a sort of matter of faith on my part since the theory is so coherent, and so powerful.[10]

The main reason to query the atheistic spin placed by Dawkins on evolutionary theory, however, is not the validity or otherwise of arguments about irreducible complexity. It is the assumption that this has 'destroyed the illusion of design', and with it the need for God. We will see how he makes this argument in a moment, and why he is wrong. But it is worth first quoting Stephen Jay Gould, a sceptical agnostic and Harvard biologist who is unfairly rubbished in *The God Delusion*, on this point:

> Either half my colleagues are enormously stupid, or else the science of Darwinism is fully compatible with conventional religious beliefs – and equally compatible with atheism.[11]

---

[10] From BBC2's *The Final Hour*, 14th November 2005.

[11] Gould, 'Impeaching a Self-Appointed Judge'. McGrath, *The Twilight of Atheism*, p. 111, quotes some statistical evidence from a 1996 survey that suggests Gould is hardly exaggerating: 40 per cent of the scientists interviewed said they had some religious

If Gould – not to mention the devoutly Christian scientists who believe in God-ordained evolution by natural selection, sometimes called 'theistic evolution' or 'BioLogos' – is right, then the 'illusion of design' cannot have been as destroyed by natural selection as Dawkins thinks.

The anthropic principle and cosmological improbability

This section is where Dawkins' case becomes more tenuous. In two sections, one based on the planet and one based on the cosmos as a whole, he argues that the God hypothesis is not necessary to account for the (admittedly very improbable) existence of life on earth. His argument is that the anthropic principle provides an alternative explanation for the apparent design of the cosmos and the planet, one which should be favoured for two reasons: (1) we know from Darwinian evolution that things don't have to be designed to *look* as if they have been, and therefore we should intuitively favour a non-design based explanation; (2) although life on earth is spectacularly improbable, it is less improbable than the existence of God, the 'Ultimate Boeing 747' himself, and there may be other explanations for it having occurred.

We can note initially that the second of these reasons

_____

beliefs, 40 per cent said they did not, and 20 per cent were agnostic.

is based on a poor premiss (as we saw above), and that it cannot therefore function as a backstop for any God-existence bouncers that fly over the wicketkeeper's head. We can also observe that even if Dawkins had succeeded in making the first, he would not have succeeded in establishing that 'there almost certainly is no God', to quote the rather bullish title of the chapter. He would simply have established that William Paley's argument that the appearance of design in nature proved God's existence was not ultimately convincing. Now, within a post-Enlightenment worldview in which 'Paley's argument for God's existence' has often been all-but-equated with 'the basis for believing in God's existence', this might seem like splitting hairs. But in fact, as we have commented more than once, neither the early church, nor for the most part the contemporary church, have built their belief in God on Paley's foundation.[12] Moving from possible alternative explanations for the universe's properties to confident atheism is therefore unfounded.

That said, the main problem is that Dawkins has not succeeded in his goal. There are three planks to his case:

---

[12] Romans 1:20 is sometimes held to be an exception, but Paul does not give it as a reason to believe in God; rather, he gives it to demonstrate that given that there is a God/gods (which the pagan world almost universally believed), creation tells us something about his/their attributes. On the other hand, Hebrews 11:3 makes clear that, since we cannot go back there and check how the world came about, believing that it was created is ultimately a matter of faith (which, as the rest of the chapter suggests, we hold on quite different grounds).

his citing of the anthropic principle as an alternative to creation; his analogy between Darwinian evolution and cosmology; and the alternative explanations he offers for the emergence of life. Each is unconvincing.

It is fairly cheeky to argue that the anthropic principle is an alternative to creation. The anthropic principle, strictly, is simply a statement of fact: the fine-tuning of the planet we live on, and the emergence of life, are statistically very improbable, but we are only here thinking about them because they happened in the first place. There are then three main explanations for the anthropic principle offered: (a) God or another intelligent designer, (b) an astonishing coincidence, or (c) a multiplicity of universes, sometimes known as the 'multiverse' theory. Dawkins may or may not be right that (a) is less likely than (b) or (c), but to say that (a) is an alternative to the anthropic principle itself is ridiculous. It is an explanation for it, not a rival version of events. In the opening scene of Tom Stoppard's play, *Rosencrantz and Guildenstern are Dead*, an obviously impossible sequence of flipped coins come down heads. Guildenstern, the more aware of the characters, is concerned about the ontological implications, since he realises the coincidence explanation, (b) above, strains credibility beyond breaking point.[13] In this analogy, the anthropic principle

---

[13] Stoppard, *Rosencrantz and Guildenstern are Dead* (New York: Grove Press 1991). It is taken as indicative of Rosencrantz's naivety that he does not comment on the 'clearly impossible' situation. He who has ears, let him hear.

corresponds to the row of heads, and should be taken as the problem, not one possible solution. It is then up to Guildenstern, Dawkins and the rest of us to decide on (a), (b) or (c).

Dawkins, then, is really presenting (a), creation by God, as an alternative to (b), staggering coincidence or (c), the multiverse theory. His basis for rejecting (a) on cosmology is built on an extrapolation from Darwinian natural selection: the existence of life in the first place, the favourable conditions of our planet, and the emergence of things like eucaryotic cells and consciousness all look designed, but then so did complex life until Darwin – so we should leave the benefit of the doubt firmly with materialistic scientific explanations, on the basis that we will eventually find one. Crucially, however, his analogy breaks down. An agnostic materialist would have believed in design before Darwin because there was no real alternative; nobody had articulated ways in which complex life could have come about without design. But the same is far from true with cosmology. Over a century of detailed searching has brought about numerous proposed alternatives to design. Design, then, does not hold the floor in the absence of any alternatives, but because a number of lines of enquiry have revealed the origin of life by chance to be astronomically unlikely.

It is worth reminding ourselves of just how unlikely, because Dawkins muddies the waters a little on this point. The 'monkeys typing out Shakespeare' picture is often quoted to suggest that, if enough time passes, life will eventually result, but it is less often noted that it would take a monkey 7.2 trillion trillion trillion trillion trillion trillion trillion years just to type the first verse of Psalm 23, and that a DNA string contains rather more information: as much as the *Encyclopædia Britannica*, apparently. It is not surprising to find that Dawkins has little time for Fred Hoyle, since he was a scientist and a non-Christian who continually pointed out the Emperor's lack of clothes on this issue,[14] but Hoyle argued that the chance of obtaining a single protein by chance combination was the same as filling the solar system with blind men, and them all solving a Rubik's Cube simultaneously. His basis for saying so was that there are only 10^{80} atoms in the known universe, yet the chance of an enzyme being formed was somewhere around 1 in $10^{40,000}$. Harold Morowitz, another non-Christian evolutionary scientist and a professor of Biophysics at Yale, estimated the probability of life by chance at 1 in $10^{340,000,000}$. So when Dawkins writes the following, it is not clear whether he is ignorant of these estimates or deliberately neglecting to mention them:

If the odds of life originating spontaneously on a planet

---

[14] I wonder if there was a wry smile when Dawkins wrote the following of Hoyle: 'At an intellectual level, I suppose he understood natural selection. But perhaps you need to be steeped in natural selection, immersed in it, swim about in it, before you can truly appreciate its power' (Dawkins, p. 117).

were a billion to one against, nevertheless that stupefyingly improbable event would still happen on a billion planets.[15]

Clearly, it is a bit misleading to talk as if the odds were a billion to one. Note, incidentally, that despite his loud disapproval of people appealing to 'chance', this sort of statement is exactly that: the argument that, given enough places and enough time, life will arise by chance (it has to have arisen by chance, since the mechanism of natural selection, as Dawkins is at pains to explain, does not apply).[16] We can get lost in the maths on this point, but we can safely suggest that (1) if the fine-tuning of the earth is sensationally improbable in itself, and (2) if, even given a planet with water and sunlight, the emergence of life is 1 in $10^{340,000,000}$, or even 1 in $10^{40,000}$, and (3) if the development of the eucaryotic cell was 'an even more momentous, difficult and statistically improbable step',[17] and (4) if the origin of consciousness was 'another major gap whose bridging was of the same order of improbability',[18] then it is laughable to refer to

---

[15] Dawkins, p. 138.

[16] His delineation of these two different approaches is admirably clear; see Dawkins, pp.139–140. However, it undermines somewhat the angry criticism of Fred Hoyle he gave in *The Blind Watchmaker*, repeated in *The God Delusion*, where he implies that the Boeing 747 argument can be defeated through Darwinian evolution, which is emphatically not a 'chance' process. Hoyle, like Morowitz, was talking about the origin of life in the first place, and it is thus slightly dishonest to suggest that the argument can be defeated by invoking natural selection.

[17] Dawkins, p. 140.   [18] Dawkins, p. 140.

all this as 'some luck' which can be explained by positing 'billions of planets'.[19] The universe is very large and very old, to be sure, but it would need to be quadrillions of times larger and older to make life by chance even slightly credible. To return to our three main explanations for the anthropic principle, it appears that (b), unthinkably large coincidence, is absurd in the light of the data we have.

Perhaps it is for this reason that Dawkins, rather unexpectedly, transitions at this point to defend option (c), the multiverse theory. Laudably, he is quite honest about the need for a more satisfying explanation than option (b):

Why did it have to be the kind of universe which seems almost as if, in the words of the theoretical physicist Freeman Dyson, it 'must have known we were coming'? The philosopher John Leslie uses the analogy of a man sentenced to death by firing squad. It is just possible that all ten men of the firing squad will miss their victim. With hindsight, the survivor who finds himself in a position to reflect upon his luck can cheerfully say, 'Well, obviously they all missed, or I wouldn't be here thinking about it.' But he could still, forgivably, wonder why they all missed, and toy with the hypothesis that they were bribed, or drunk. This objection can be answered by the suggestion, which Martin Rees himself supports, that there are many universes, co-existing like bubbles of foam, in a 'multiverse' (or 'megaverse', as Leonard Susskind prefers to call it).[20]

---

[19] Dawkins, p. 141.   [20] Dawkins, p. 144–145.

It is odd that, having fought hard against speculation and for a materialistic, scientific simplicity throughout *The God Delusion*, Dawkins proceeds to cut himself so badly with Ockham's razor. The weaknesses of his argument here are so obvious that it is remarkable to find him making it – it may suggest a naïve credulity in any explanation offered, as long as it is nothing like the God of the Bible. There is no evidence whatever for such an idea, as indeed there could not be. It is an almost infinitely complex theory, which can be attacked on exactly the same grounds as those on which Dawkins attacks theism, yet without any of the explanatory power that theism offers. By the time Dawkins attempts to respond to this objection, by saying that the multiverse theory is statistically more probable than an intelligent God, he has built so many castles in the air that it is hard to know how to attack them. As one reviewer put it:

> His polemic would come rather more convincingly from a man who was a little less arrogantly triumphalistic about science (there are a mere one or two gestures in the book to its fallibility), and who could refrain from writing sentences like 'this objection [to a particular scientific view] can be answered by the suggestion . . . that there are many universes,' as though a suggestion constituted a scientific rebuttal.[21]

The final line of defence against those who would scoff that this theory creates more problems than it solves,

---

[21] Review by Terry Eagleton in the *London Review of Books*, 19th October 2006.

unsurprisingly, is the reiterated claim that God is the Ultimate Boeing 747, since his existence from a place of non-existence is supremely unlikely. As we have seen, this argument is unsustainable in any event. But even if it was not, it would surely reflect the paucity of options (b) and (c) in that Dawkins could only opt for them by misrepresenting option (a).

Dawkins is not alone in his preference for materialist explanations, no matter how far-fetched, over theistic ones. But each example just shows how entrenched is the (manifestly false) belief in certain quarters that science and God cannot co-exist. Francis Crick, who helped discover the structure of DNA, avoided believing in God by arguing that life had been sent to earth from another planet – which, of course, solves nothing.[22] Dawkins' colleague Peter Atkins gave such a bizarre argument for multiverses against John Polkinghorne and me in 1999 that he somehow managed to lose a debate on creation on the floor of the Cambridge Union.[23] The Harvard biologist Richard Lewontin, though not speaking about multiverses, might as well have been when he declared, seemingly without irony:

> We take the side of science in spite of the patent absurdity of some of its constructs . . . because we have a prior commitment, a commitment to materialism. It is not that the

[22] Francis Crick, *Life Itself:* Its Origin and Nature (New York: Simon and Schuster 1981).

[23] The motion was 'This house believes in creation'.

methods and institutions of science somehow compel us to accept a material explanation of the phenomenal world, but, on the contrary, that we are forced by our a priori adherence to material causes to create an apparatus of investigation and a set of concepts that produce material explanations, no matter how counterintuitive, no matter how mystifying to the uninitiated. Moreover, that materialism is absolute, for we cannot allow a Divine Foot in the door.[24]

Materialism, eh? 'There's a lion in the street!' (Proverbs 26:13).[25]

---

[24] Richard Lewontin, *The New York Review*, 9th January 1997, p. 31.

[25] This comment is unashamedly stolen from Wright, *Resurrection*, p. 713, on Robert Morgan's attempt to explain the resurrection in rationalist terms.

The fool says in his heart, 'There is no God.'

Psalm 14:1

7

Conclusion

The *God Delusion* is stimulating, well written, amusing and combative. It gathers together every available arrow into the atheist's quiver, and fires them at theism with a combination of rhetorical skill and a good sense of humour. If, as I anticipate, it sells better than rival atheist manifestos,[1] it will be because it is written by an eminent scientist and a strong communicator, who has for many years been on the front line in attacking belief in God. So whether one is a believer or not, it is worth taking seriously.

Yet when studied carefully, the thesis of the book does not hold water. When the polemic is stripped away, and

---

[1] I exclude the books of Sam Harris from this assessment, because Harris mainly directs his attention, not at belief in God, but at a particularly virulent strain of fundamentalism. One wonders whether he considered replacing the title *The End of Faith* with *The End of Fundamentalism*, but decided against it because fundamentalism is so clearly alive and well – not least in the work of Richard Dawkins.

the irrelevant and unsubstantiated side issues are put on one side, there are only four lines of argument left. And not only do none of these cover the elephant in the room, the resurrection of Jesus, but they also fall in their own right. The strident anti-supernaturalism that pervades the book is never substantiated, and is open to the charge of cooking the evidence in advance; the brief logical argument is both facile and inadequate; the attack on Scripture is littered with mistakes and misrepresentations, which severely undermine the case being made; and in the scientific section, where we would expect Dawkins to be strongest, both the premisses of and the appeals to unprovable theories render his argument weak. In fact, the selective use of evidence and – to be blunt – poor research that characterise several sections of *The God Delusion* could lead one to the conclusion that Dawkins is just as fundamentalist as the religious fanatics he is seeking to discredit. They certainly do him no favours.

Books like *The God Delusion* will continue to be written, no doubt. Scientists, philosophers and journalists will continue sniping at religion, some with erudition and balance, some with populism and mockery, and some with a combination of these. Not all of them will deserve lengthy responses or demand national attention. But they will all need to be met by reasoned argument, and the questioning of the premisses and methods of a post-Enlightenment secular worldview that, while very common, is not *a priori* entitled to intellectual hegemony. The answer is not to drift into a sort of private piety, closed to question because it is so devoutly held. Nor is it to resort to a liberal take-it-or-leave-it philosophy, whereby we keep the bits of Christianity our culture accepts and throw away the rest, with the result that the gospel becomes ever smaller and more irrelevant. It is to fight fire with fire: to challenge the foolishness of the world with the wisdom of the cross, safe in the knowledge that there is nothing new under the sun,[2] and that a resurrected Saviour is no less controversial or more problematic in London today than it was in Athens in the AD 50s. We must not bypass the head nor hide under the bed. We must listen; we must debate; and we must fight intellectual battles, waging war on every argument that sets itself up against the knowledge of Christ, and taking each thought captive to him.[3]

As for Dawkins, he remains an enigma. No matter how confident he is in his final chapter that science can offer the consolation currently provided by religion, and despite his apparent frustration with the idea of an infinite God, he may still be questing, as implied in an interview following the publication of *The God Delusion*:

> When we started out and we were talking about the origins of the universe and the physical constants, I provided what I thought were cogent arguments against a supernatural intelligent designer. But it does seem to me to be a worthy

---

[2] Ecclesiastes 1:9.
[3] 2 Corinthians 10:5.

idea. Refutable – but nevertheless grand and big enough to be worthy of respect . . . If there is a God, it's going to be a whole lot bigger and a whole lot more incomprehensible than anything that any theologian of any religion has ever proposed.[4]

Like Einstein, then, Dawkins' problem seems to be that the God or gods he has heard described are simply not big enough. To be fair, if the God of the Bible was the small, petulant, Freudian superego that Dawkins imagines, I would not believe in him either. But Yahweh, the God of Abraham, Isaac and Jacob, is far larger and more glorious than Dawkins imagines, as I have explained elsewhere:

No pictures are sufficient to express the full truth about him, not even biblical ones . . . In intercession, he is both the one praying and the one being prayed to. In justice, he is the policeman, judge, jury, defence lawyer, and the one who receives the punishment. In the tabernacle, he is both Aaron and the goat, as in an astonishing twist which no one saw coming, the high priest and the sacrifice on the altar turn out to be the same person. In the family, he is father, mother, son and husband. He is unknowable and known, invisible and revealed, lion and lamb, Prince of peace and man of war, wrathful and joyful, strength and song, holy and gracious, prophet, priest and king.[5]

---

[4] From a joint interview with Francis Collins entitled 'In Depth: The Evolution Wars' for *Time*, 5th November 2006.

[5] Andrew Wilson, *Incomparable:* Exploring the Character of God

There was once an opponent of Christianity so aggressive that he made Dawkins look very tame in comparison. He fought believers with all his might, both intellectually and physically, and dedicated his life to ridding the world of the blight of Christianity. Yet as he eventually found out, the size and holiness and love and power and truth of the God revealed in Jesus of Nazareth are incomparable. And for this reason, God is more than enough to satisfy the sceptic's soul.

> Oh, the depth of the riches and wisdom and knowledge of God! How unsearchable are his judgments and how inscrutable his ways! "For who has known the mind of the Lord, or who has been his counsellor?" "Or who has given a gift to him that he might be repaid?" For from him and through him and to him are all things. To him be glory forever. Amen.[6]

(Eastbourne: Survivor Books [Kingsway], forthcoming in June 2007).

[6] Romans 11:33–36.